JOB LOSSES IN MAJOR INDUSTRIES

Manpower Strategy Responses

by

Robert B. McKersie

Alfred P. Sloan School of Management
Massachusetts Institute of Technology
United States

and

Werner Sengenberger
Institut für Sozialwissenschaftliche Forschung
Germany

ORGANISATION FOR ECONOMIC CO-OPERATION AND DEVELOPMENT

Pursuant to article 1 of the Convention signed in Paris on 14th December, 1960, and which came into force on 30th September, 1961, the Organisation for Economic Co-operation and Development (OECD) shall promote policies designed:

- to achieve the highest sustainable economic growth and employment and a rising standard of living in Member countries, while maintaining financial stability, and thus to contribute to the development of the world economy;
- to contribute to sound economic expansion in Member as well as non-member countries in the process of economic development; and
- to contribute to the expansion of world trade on a multilateral, non-discriminatory basis in accordance with international obligations.

The Signatories of the Convention on the OECD are Austria, Belgium, Canada, Denmark, France, the Federal Republic of Germany, Greece, Iceland, Ireland, Italy, Luxembourg, the Netherlands, Norway, Portugal, Spain, Sweden, Switzerland, Turkey, the United Kingdom and the United States. The following countries acceded subsequently to this Convention (the dates are those on which the instruments of accession were deposited): Japan (28th April, 1964), Finland (28th January, 1969), Australia (7th June, 1971) and New Zealand (29th May, 1973).

The Socialist Federal Republic of Yugoslavia takes part in certain work of the OECD (agreement of 28th October, 1961).

Publié en français sous le titre:

**LES SUPPRESSIONS D'EMPLOIS
DANS L'INDUSTRIE**

Industrial societies continually face structural change. Movements of contraction and expansion, disinvestment and reinvestment, internal or external redeployment of capital, and elimination and creation of jobs, occur in different sectors and undertakings with varying scope and pace.

Recent years have seen extensive restructuring in certain economic sectors under the individual or combined effects of declining demand, technical change and changing trade patterns. Many basic sectors (iron and steel, shipbuilding, textiles and the motor industry) are currently facing severe recession and are engaged in far-reaching conversions entailing massive job elimination.

This report deals with large-scale dislocations of employment in these sectors in a number of OECD countries. It describes their significance and the consequences, economic and other, for the workers, communities and regions affected. It also discusses the structural changes which have led up to these situations, and the range of national and industrial strategies applied to respond to them. But the bulk of the report is devoted to a detailed analysis of integrative strategies and conversion programmes that seek to reconcile capital mobility with labour protection. Based on examples of such approaches - in particular in the Federal Republic of Germany and Japan - the report describes internal and external restructuring programmes. In each case it distinguishes betweeen measures focusing on job conversion and on the conversion of workers, and examines them in detail. Apart from the role of central and local governmental authorities, the report discusses the extent of worker participation in these restructuring programmes, and the problems that it poses for employers and trade unions.

The report was a contribution to the work of the OECD's Manpower and Social Affairs Committee. It is published under the responsibility of the Secretary-General. The ideas expressed are those of the authors and do not necessarily represent those of the Secretariat or of the Governments of OECD countries.

The authors would like to express their appreciation to a number of individuals and institutions for their help in preparing this study. Professors Robert Aronson, Walter Galenson, and John Windmuller of the New York State School of Industrial and Labor Relations, Cornell

University and John Hughes of Ruskin College, Oxford
University read the preliminary draft and offered sugges-
tions for improvement.

    Robert McKersie is grateful to Cornell University for
providing sabbatical leave, to the Industrial Relations
Research Unit, Warwick University, Great Britain, for
providing office space and a congenial atmosphere, and to
the Ford Foundation for providing financial assistance in
the form of a travel grant.

TABLE OF CONTENTS

Also available

THE CHALLENGE OF UNEMPLOYMENT. A Report to Labour Ministers (June 1982)
(81 82 04 1) ISBN 92-64-12332-6   166 pages   £7.60   US$17.00   F76.00

EMPLOYMENT IN THE PUBLIC SECTOR. "Document" Series (June 1982)
(81 82 03 1) ISBN 92-64-12319-9   80 pages   £3.20   US$7.25   F32.00

LABOUR SUPPLY, GROWTH CONSTRAINTS AND WORK SHARING (February 1982)
(81 82 01 1) ISBN 92-64-12279-6   68 pages   £2.90   US$6.50   F29.00

DIRECT JOB CREATION IN THE PUBLIC SECTOR (April 1980)
(81 80 03 1) ISBN 92-64-12048-3   44 pages   £2.00   US$4.50   F18.00

MANPOWER AND SOCIAL ASPECTS OF POSITIVE ADJUSTMENT POLICIES (to be published)

INTRODUCTION

This report describes, analyses and evaluates strategies, policies and measures designed and practised in various Member countries of OECD to adjust to large-scale employment dislocations.

The range of historical experience presented in this report both on employment dislocation and policy responses is limited largely to the 1970s and the turn of the 1970s to the 1980s. Starting in the recession of 1973 to 1975 most countries faced major employment declines in a number of industries as a result of generally lower economic growth, fluctuating business activity and structural reconversions in the economies. In this report we draw attention mainly to the incidence and instances of large-scale worker displacements in this period.

By focusing on declining sectors and dislocation processes the report does not deal with all employment aspects of structural change and restructuring policies. Thus, for example, the question of the quantity and quality of new employment created in the course of structural change is largely outside the perimeter of this study.

In terms of empirical coverage the report is limited to a selected number of industries and countries. The industries include textiles, steel, shipbuilding and automobiles, i.e. industries that have experienced major workforce reductions in most countries over the recent past. Country coverage extends mainly to the United States, Sweden, France, the Federal Republic of Germany, Japan and the United Kingdom with occasional reference to experience and practice in other countries. While we do not claim to present a complete survey of all of the interesting and advanced cases and developments that have occurred within the selected nations, we feel that we have caught a fair cross section of the most innovative and representative examples of adjustment policies.

The terms "employment dislocation" and "worker displacement" are used in this report as generic terms indicating significantly declining employment levels in an

enterprise or industry. While, under this definition, it
is inherent that the impending loss of jobs is fairly rapid
extensive and permanent, the definition leaves room for
various philosophies, methods and instruments for adjusting
the work force to the loss of jobs. The speed of adjustment may be fast and immediate or slow and gradual; it
may be brought about directly through lay-offs or indirectly through natural attrition, early retirements and
other "soft" measures of reduction. Moreover, adjustment
may be considered as the prime responsibility of the firm
or it may be viewed as a major area for public or state
intervention.

Though it is the aim of this report to portray and
discuss various conceivable approaches towards major job
loss in terms of the strategies, instruments and measures,
we give special attention to positive modes of accommodating the problem of excess labour. Thus, one of the
positive strategies for dealing with impending abrupt dislocation is to convert the situation into a gradual displacement process. Hence we shall detail the latter
mechanism and its corresponding policy instruments since
we see it as a preferable alternative.

I

THE EXTENT OF LARGE-SCALE EMPLOYMENT DISLOCATIONS

The process of structural change and worker displacement - Before delving into a discussion of the types of basic changes that have been occurring across industries and countries, it is appropriate to say a few words about the concept of structural change: what Schumpeter called the Creative Distruction (and reinvestment) of Capital. Structural change in industrial societies proceeds by the elimination and creation of jobs. To the extent that the newly created jobs are more productive than the old ones, structural change is a highly desirable process, and as part of the process of economic growth becomes the basis for improvement in economic well-being and the standard of living.

However, structural changes also pose various threats and may cause serious social damage depending on how the changes come about. As historical experience has shown, the changes frequently do not proceed smoothly and evenly, but tend to evolve in rather discontinuous and non-linear fashion. Expansion of employment in growing sectors, industries or regions may not compensate in the short run or even middle term for the losses of jobs in contracting sectors and locations, with the result that large-scale structural imbalances emerge.

The process of employment contraction and expansion has at least two dimensions, a temporal and a spatial one. In a temporal sense, the creation of new jobs may not keep pace with the decline of jobs. Such dys-synchronous development is especially likely to occur if the displacement process emerges suddenly, rapidly or abruptly, like convulsions. In a spatial sense the destruction and creation of employment may not happen in the same location, leaving imbalances across areas, regions or countries.

The less synchronous, the less locationally balanced and the larger the scope of industrial reconversion, the greater will be the potential for major employment dislocations with economic and social damage inflicted upon workers, firms and communities.

11

The most dramatic expression of these dislocations are plant closures and large-scale dismissal of workers. The impact of such action tends to be particularly serious if the declining industry is concentrated in a particular area and if the area has no industrial diversity (industrial monostructure).

Historical backdrop - Worker displacement is a process that goes on continuously. Businesses are constantly going through the life cycle of birth and death. For the most part these changes occur gradually and affect small-scale enterprises.(1) Consequently, the scope of workforce displacement at any one point in time and for any locality is relatively limited. Thus, while the aggregate figures of jobs lost through the "churning" of the economic system seem large, when broken down on a micro basis (for a particular labour market for a particular point in time) the numbers may not be that devastating. For example, it has been noted that during the decade of the 1970s, the New England economy experienced a loss of approximately one million jobs.(2) However, in that same period almost as many jobs were created and, consequently, this region of the United States has remained in relatively good economic health.

Before detailing the extent of large-scale displacement, it is instructive to examine some industries that have experienced substantial work-force reductions without extensive dislocation over the past several decades, a significant contrast to the current situation gripping so many industries in so many countries. An interesting industry for this purpose is coal, since it frequently occurs in isolated locations and, as a result, has the potential for creating substantial structural unemployment. In the case of United Kingdom coalmining, between 1960 and 1970, manpower in the industry dropped from 602,000 to 287,000. However, for this large reduction in employment (over 300,000) the number of redundancies amounted to slightly over 60,000 and most of these occurred during

_____

1. Consider the background picture for manufacturing in Scotland - a section of Britain that has incurred considerable work-force displacement of the sort that we will be interested in considering in this report. Between 1966 and 1975 manufacturing plants in Scotland experienced closure rates anywhere from 1 to 4 per cent per annum. Thus, over a ten-year period one-quarter to one-third of the plants in existence would no longer be in existence. The highest incidence of failure occurred for small plants and for plants shortly after their arrival on the scene. Robert A. Henderson, "An Analysis of Closure Amongst Scottish Manufacturing Plants Between 1966 and 1975", Scottish Journal of Political Economy, Vol. 27, No. 2, June 1980, pp. 152-174.
2. Barry Bluestone and Benjamin Harrison, Capital and Communities, The Progressive Alliance, Washington, D.C., 1980.

the latter phase of the programme when normal and early retirements were less available to the Coal Board as a solution.(3)

A similar experience occurred in the Limburg coal fields of the Netherlands in the 1960s when coalmining employment was reduced by 30,000 (starting from a base of 44,000) with normal and early retirement handling slightly over 10,000 and other employment about 16,000 individuals.

The 1960s also saw massive reductions in employment in the United Kingdom and the United States railroading. Between 1963 and 1973 employment in British Rail dropped from 477,000 to 230,000; two-thirds of this reduction came about as a result of normal and early retirement as well as special redundancy payments.(4)

For the United States railroads, employment in the late 1940s stood at over one million workers; by the late 1970s it had dropped to approximately 500,000. Almost all of this reduction occurred through normal attrition, with only a small number of workers having been severed involuntarily.

The same story of dramatic rundowns in employment (occurring on a gradual basis) could be told for the docks in the United States, the United Kingdom and other countries, as well as for a variety of other industries. For example, in a ten-year period between 1969 and 1979 the United States Postal Service experienced a drop in employment from 656,000 to 585,000 without any layoffs.

Characteristics of the industries just mentioned - The industries that have gone through large-scale work-force displacements and handled them in their stride have a number of common characteristics. Generally, they are either owned by government or are in close relationship to the government via subsidies and other financial support programmes.(5) The industries tend to be oriented towards domestic markets - sometimes exclusively so, such as post offices and railroads. This combination of being isolated from foreign competition and being supported by government financing enables the changes to be phased gradually so that the shifts do not become convulsions.

---

3. M.I.A. Bulmer, "Mining Redundancy: A Case Study of the Working of the R.P.A. in the Durham Coalfield", Industrial Relations, Winter 1971, Vol. 2, No. 4, pp. 3-21.
4. George H. Hildebrand, "Industrial Relations Under Continuous Strain: British Railways Since Nationalisation", in Union Power and Public Policy, Ed. David Lipsky, New York State School of Industrial and Labor Relations, Ithaca, New York, 1975.
5. In the case of the run down in coalmining in Belgium, the government authorised the industry to release 100 men a month with the government paying for all the losses.

It should also be recognised that the decline in employment can take place in small doses due to the nature of the technology and the way in which the work force is dispersed, as is the case for railroads and mines. A single coal mine may not employ more than several hundred workers and its closing then can be phased along a time continuum. Such is not the case with a steel mill which may employ 4,000 or 5,000 workers and where it is difficult to phase its demise in quite the same way as would be true of railroads and the mines.

A SELECTIVE ACCOUNT OF MAJOR EMPLOYMENT DISLOCATIONS

We now portray instances of major employment dislocations in selected countries and industries. For this purpose we present two kinds of information. In the following tables (Tables 1 to 4) we show indicators of production and employment changes for each year from 1970 to 1980 for the textiles, basic iron and steel, ship-building and repairing, and motor vehicles industries in the United States, Japan, Sweden, Germany, France and the United Kingdom. In a second step we list, for largely the same selection of industries and countries, some more detailed information of instances of major loss in the industry as a whole and in particular companies. We have chosen these industries mainly for two reasons. One is that the selected industries belong to those which have been most stricken by economic declines during the 1970s. Second, the selection represents a good mix of different dates at which major employment dislocation set in during the 1970s.

It should be noted that the economic indicators applied here give only a very rough approximation of the scope of dislocation effects. Given different national policy interventions and institutional arrangements in the various countries, registered employment as well as unemployment data do not reveal the true extent of excess labour. For example, policies of temporary employment maintenance have been applied to a substantially different degree in the countries and industries under consideration. Similarly, production figures may reflect temporary efforts at holding up production levels through public subsidization and may not be a good indicator of the industry's future if, for instance, these subsidies cannot be continued in light of more permanent problems of decline.

Textiles

According to an estimate of the Commission of the European Communities, the textile industries of the

14

Table 1

INDICATORS OF PRODUCTION AND EMPLOYMENT IN THE TEXTILE INDUSTRY IN SELECTED COUNTRIES
1970-1980

1975 = 100

	1970	1971	1972	1973	1974	1975	1976	1977	1978	1979	1980
United States											
Production	95.1	97.9	106	112	107	100	113	116	117	118	114
Employment	-	-	115	117	111	100	106	105	106	103	99.4
Japan											
Production		-	-	-	106	100	108	106	107	108	107
Employment		-	-	-	100	100	99.6	95.6	88.0	90.3	89.0
Sweden											
Production	110	102	103	108	108	100	96	83	72	72	70
Employment	-	-	-	-	102	100	90	81	75	70	67
Germany											
Production	111	113	116	111	103	100	103	101	98.2	99.6	96.2
Employment	-	-	-	-	-	100	96.4	95.5	93.0	91.3	88.9
France											
Production	98.7	107	113	111	110	100	106	102	98.8	101	96.4
Employment	110	107	109	108	105	100	96.0	93.6	89.8	86.8	84.3
United Kingdom											
Production	-	-		110	103	100	101	102	102	100	85.1
Employment	-	-		-	-	100	-	96.4	93.7	92.1	83.3

Source: OECD, Indicators of Industrial Activity, Special Computations.

15

Table 2

INDICATORS OF PRODUCTION AND EMPLOYMENT IN THE BASIC IRON AND STEEL INDUSTRIES
IN SELECTED COUNTRIES
1970-1980

1975 = 100

	1970	1971	1972	1973	1974	1975	1976	1977	1978	1979	1980
United States											
Production	109	100	112	128	125	100	109	108	118	118	95.7
Employment	-	-	103	110	113	100	100	101	103	106	92.4
Japan											
Production	94.2	91.2	98.7	119	117	100	110	108	110	123	124
Employment	-	-	-	-	101	100	96.3	93.5	89.6	85.7	84.2
Sweden											
Production	93.7	91.4	91.6	100	107	100	89.5	80.0	83.2	90.0	84.3
Employment	-	-	-	-	105	100	97.8	91.6	75.1	85.3	83.4
Germany											
Production	111	99.7	104	119	126	100	103	98.1	102	112	107
Employment	-	-	-	-	-	100	88.9	88.7	85.3	84.9	85.0
France											
Production	108	104	107	115	122	100	108	104	108	112	111
Employment	96.8	98.0	96.6	96.9	99.3	100	98.5	96.2	89.2	82.1	75.0
United Kingdom											
Production	133	119	119	128	115	100	104	103	101	102	66.8
Employment	-	-	-	-	-	100	-	95.0	89.2	84.7	74.4

Source: OECD, Indicators of Industrial Activity, Special Computations.

Table 3

INDICATORS OF PRODUCTION AND EMPLOYMENT IN THE SHIPBUILDING AND REPAIRING INDUSTRY
IN SELECTED COUNTRIES
1970-1980

1975 = 100

	1970	1971	1972	1973	1974	1975	1976	1977	1978	1979	1980
United States											
Production	70.9	71.3	85.4	90.3	96.9	100	108	111	122	110	108
Employment	–	–	99.8	102	104	100	111	113	114	114	109
Japan											
Production	–	–	–	–	110	100	80.1	66.8	28.7	29.9	39.0
Employment	–	–	–	–	99.4	100	96.7	91.1	80.1	67.0	63.2
Sweden											
Production	66.9	69.5	79.6	84.0	86.3	100	93.4	78.0	64.5	55.6	52.6
Employment	–	–	–	–	91.4	100	93.9	87.5	80.4	73.6	61.1
Germany											
Production	80.3	80.2	79.4	82.0	90.4	100	96.3	90.0	79.6	74.4	77.9
Employment	–	–	–	–	–	100	95.3	91.4	83.6	74.4	72.9
France											
Production	93.2	96.0	97.2	97.7	98.2	100	100	98.2	95.2	93.6	94.5
Employment	–	–	–	–	–	100	–	–	–	–	–
United Kingdom											
Production	–	–	–	95.4	98.9	100	96.5	93.5	86.4	78.1	67.8
Employment	–	–	–	–	–	100	–	99.5	99.1	94.8	85.5

Source: OECD, <u>Indicators of Industrial Activity</u>, Special Computations.

Table 4

INDICATORS OF PRODUCTION AND EMPLOYMENT IN THE MOTOR VEHICLE INDUSTRY IN SELECTED COUNTRIES
1970-1980

1975=100

	1970	1971	1972	1973	1974	1975	1976	1977	1978	1979	1980
United States											
Production	83.1	107	122	140	115	100	128	145	153	144	107
Employment	-	-	112	125	114	100	113	121	130	127	92.4
Japan											
Production	-	-	-	-	94.5	100	113	123	137	150	170
Employment	-	-	-	-	103	100	99.9	102	104	99.7	103
Sweden											
Production	-	-	-	-	-	-	-	-	-	-	-
Employment	-	-	-	-	93.6	100	101	96.9	96.4	104	110
Germany											
Production	99.6	101	102	110	95.6	100	112	119	121	128	121
Employment	-	-	-	-	-	100	105	112	117	121	121
France											
Production	83.4	91.3	101	109	105	-	117	122	123	127	121
Employment	86.1	91.9	95.2	101	103	100	104	107	107	106	104
United Kingdom											
Production	-	-	-	119	111	100	100	107	104	99.3	85.9
Employment	-	-	-	-	-	100	-	102	103	100	91.6

Source: OECD, Indicators of Industrial Activity, Special Computations.

Community countries during the 1980s could lose half of their current employment, amounting to one million dis- placees, as a result of import competition from developing countries, from the United States and from Eastern European countries. This expected reduction of the European textile industry comes on top of substantial previous decline. Between 1974 and 1980, about 4,000 firms were forced to close and 710,000 jobs were destroyed.

During the last three years the artificial and syn- thetic fibres industry in several European countries has been among the worst affected sectors in terms of job loss.

Japan - Some of the large Japanese textile manu- facturers cut down their work forces during the depression period of 1974-1975. Kanebo closed five plants for six months, transferring 1,650 employees to other plants out- side the textile division. Yunichika shut down three of its plants and reduced operations in six others and as a result, 3,000 workers were on temporary lay-off. The Toyo Spinning Company encouraged its employees to resign volun- tarily, hoping to achieve a 15 per cent reduction of its labour force.

United Kingdom - Recent reports have suggested that a good fraction of the 450,000 jobs in the textile indus- try could be at risk, as a result of the substantially increased imports. Late in 1980, for example, ICI decided to close two of its fibre plants, thereby necessitating the redundancy of 4,000 individuals.

Germany - The textile industry passed through an intensive period of restructuring during the 1970s. Be- tween 1970 and 1979 the number of firms declined from 2,400 to 1,700; and employment receded from 500,000 to 300,000. Between 1970 and 1976 the German textile indus- try was the frontrunner among all German industries in losing jobs. Imports of textile products climbed steadily to a level of 45 per cent in 1973. At the same time, the proportion of exported goods increased as well, from 21 to 37 per cent; finally, in spite of the greatly reduced employment, real output was about 9 per cent higher at the end of the 1970s.

The transition period was marked by product and pro- cess innovation and product specialisation, increasing both the capital intensity and the productivity of the in- dustry considerably. The adjustment of employment was associated with relocation, plant closures and attrition of work forces. The contraction hit some of the most disadvantaged and remote regions (like border areas), and contributed to a growing regional imbalance in the labour market. Moreover, it had a very negative impact on female and unskilled workers.

France - Approximately 600,000 individuals work in the textile and clothing industry. Many have been dis-placed as small firms have been forced to close as a re-sult of tough competition, often from imports. The over-all impact has not been as severe as in some other countries of the Common Market, since the industry has maintained a vital core as a number of large companies have pursued acquisitions and mergers to fill out their product lines, thereby retaining substantial marketing strength.

For small and medium-sized companies the impact has been severe and has affected certain textile towns quite dramatically. For example, in the Vosges region, with textile employment normally averaging 21,000 workers, 3,000 jobs were lost during 1980, and in the spring of the subsequent year another 6,000 workers were on short time.(6)

Steel Industry

The steel industry in most of the advanced industrial nations is in a state of crisis. The cyclical downturn in 1980 took place against a structural crisis in the industry which dates back to the recession of 1973-74. Prices for steel, previously fairly stable, became vola-tile towards the end of the 1970s. At the same time production costs have increased as a result of higher costs for iron ore and energy and sharply reduced rates of capacity utilisation, leading to lower profitability of operations and substantial losses in many quarters of the industry.

Steel production within OECD nations, which in 1974 reached an all-time peak of almost 458 million tons, has since ranged between 384 and 433 million tons. The latest survey by OECD shows that only 69 per cent of the OECD steel capacity was used in 1980 and 1981, implying a gap of about 115 million tons between actual and poten-tial production.(7)

In spite of major attempts to maintain plant and employment through heavy subsidization in several European countries, extensive job losses have occurred during the recent past and significant reductions are planned for the near future in most steel-production countries. Be-tween 1974 and 1981 total employment in the OECD's steel industry fell by 400,00 or 20 per cent.

----

6. Financial Times, 8 April 1981.
7. The Steel Market in 1981 and the Outlook for 1982, OECD, Paris, 1982.

The downturn of the steel industry has created serious labour market imbalances to particular steel-producing areas and regions. In spite of partial relocations of iron and steel plants from the traditional coal or ore-based centres to coastal areas, a heavy concentration of steel production has remained in such areas as Youngstown (Ohio), Lorraine in France, West Midlands and South Wales in Britain, the Ruhr and Saar districts in Germany and the Basque region around Bilbao in Spain. Frequently, the economic plight of these regions is exacerbated by previous or present decline of the coalmining and shipbuilding industries.

United States - Some 46,000 jobs were lost during 1979 and 1980. At the end of 1981, employment was about 100,000 less than 1974 (i.e. 20 per cent). US Steel announced in 1979 that it intended to close a number of operations involving a total of 13,000 employees. Bethlehem Steel has laid off 15,000 workers and is operating at about half of capacity in its remaining facilities.

Nationwide, the 1980 unemployment rate in the basic steel industry amounted to about 25 per cent with pockets of unemployment considerably higher than the average. One of the cities most affected by the shutdown of steel mills has been Youngstown, Ohio. US Steel and Youngstown Sheet and Tube have closed four large mills, producing a job loss of 10,000 and a local unemployment rate of 13.2 per cent in early 1981.

Japan - From 1974 to 1981 employment decreased from 324,000 to 270,000 (17 per cent). While portions of the industry maintained normal operating rates and employment levels, substantial weeding out of old facilities occurred during the late 1970s. For example, Nippon Steel, one of the largest steel producers closed a major plant in its Kamaishi complex during 1979 to 1980. While most of the steel workers affected by the shutdown (approximately 500 persons) were handled by attrition, a much larger number of workers in subcontracting and other firms related to the steel industry experienced redundancy. For example, 800 workers at an iron ore mine in Kamaishi lost employment. Significantly, the mayor of Kamaishi led a march of 5,000 protesting the "rationalisation plans".

Europe - The basic iron and steel industry of the EEC countries shed close to 223,000 jobs between 1974 and 1981, so that an employment of about 577,000 remained at the end of 1981. But it still appears much too big, with only 60 per cent of its capacity in use. During 1980 alone the job loss amounted to 70,000. The Commission of the EEC developed a plan, effective by 1 October 1980, to deal with the crisis which affects all Member countries, which prescribes production quotas for all steel-producing companies.

21

United Kingdom - The steel industry lost over 100,000 jobs between 1974 and 1981. During the year of 1980 employment declined by about 20,000 to arrive at 134,000 and, in 1981, a further fall of employment by 38,000 occurred.

The British Steel Corporation, the nationalised steel producer in Great Britain, announced that they were going to cut employment by 52,000 in 1980, but in fact these losses will be taking place over a longer period. In the Talbot Works in South Wales nearly half of the 12,000 workers have been laid off.

Germany - Employment in steel has declined by 38,000 (16 per cent) since 1974 and there is the prospect of further decline at plant locations which are at a dis- advantage due to high transportation costs (including the Saar and Dortmund areas, Salzgitter and Eastern Bavaria) and in the less technologically advanced facilities.

In the Saar steel-making district a loss of 5,000 jobs was encountered between 1975 and 1978 at the Röchling- Burback Company. At the Neunkircher Eisenwerke employ- ment was reduced by 900 in 1977 and another loss of 3,700 jobs is scheduled for the 1980-1982 period following a planned partial closure of the facilities.

Management at the Hoesch-Werke of Dortmund has recently closed down a steel mill and has scheduled the shutdown of two further mills using the obsolete Siemens- Martin technique. The abandoned mills are to be replaced by an oxygen plant which would lower total capacity by about 25 per cent and would generate a job reduction of 4,200.

The decline of the iron and steel industry along with the shrinkage of coalmining in the Ruhr and Saar areas has drained the industrial capacity of two of Germany's previous industrial heartlands. In the Ruhr district approximately 500,000 jobs were lost between 1958 and 1974, whereas the number of newly created jobs was only about 170,000.

France - The steel industry is undergoing a re- structuring process concerning both geographical re- location of the industry from the Lorraine to the areas of Dunkirk, Fos and Nancy-Thionville and modernisation and rationalisation of production. In 1981 the level of employment was down to 100,000 from 155,000 in 1976. The adjustment process has produced a major and serious crisis in the industry, involving worker unrest and social protests in the communities in the north and north-east affected by the reductions. The Lorraine steel industry, which employed around 100,000 workers in the early 1960s, now has no more than 70,000 employees. The plight of the region was made more severe by the loss of jobs in the textile and coalmining industries. Employment in these industries shrunk by one half over the past 25 years.

Sweden - Employment in the steel industry declined by 20 per cent between 1976 and 1981, but major shutdowns of operations have been avoided so far. Over the next ten years, however, a substantial permanent reduction of jobs is projected, including the partial and complete closure of a number of activities. In 1981 job loss of 2,600 reduced the work force to 41,000 by the end of the year.

Shipbuilding Industry

For several years the shipbuilding industry on a worldwide basis has been undergoing far-reaching structural changes to adjust to the rapidly decreasing market. During this period, shipbuilding nations under the pressure of strong unions and employer lobbies have increasingly taken up measures to improve the national industry's competitive position. Subsidies have been provided to maintain both production and employment.

United States - The shipbuilding industry relies primarily on government orders, hence it is small in size and relatively stable. Nevertheless, in 1976 Sun Ship, Inc. which had lost $250 million the previous year, shut down a number of its major facilities, laying off approximately 3,000 individuals.

Japan - Japan's shipbuilding industry, by far the largest in the world, has been troubled by surplus capacity and excess labour since 1975. Until about 1979 the country's seven major shipbuilding companies attempted to adjust their work forces to lower demand by "soft" reduction measures, such as recruitment freezes, transfer to departments outside of shipbuilding and natural attrition. Mitshubishi, for example, by using such measures lowered its work force in shipbuilding from 80,000 in 1975 to 68,300 in 1979.

As the slump in the industry continued and further excess of manpower became apparent, the shipbuilders considered further and more drastic efforts to cut back employment. In 1979 Mitshubishi found ways to reduce employment by another 10,000 workers through natural wastage, transfers and early retirement. During the same year the other five large companies revised their reduction programmes as well, amounting to a combined total of planned reduction by 22,750, a large downsizing compared to the 58,000 workers employed in their shipbuilding divisions.

All in all, the displacement of workers from the shipbuilding industry in Japan has been of monumental proportions. Between December 1974 and June 1979 employment in the industry fell from 274,000 to 157,000, a drop of 117,000. Almost half of the reduction came from contract workers, who are mostly piece-workers and who for the most part exhibit high mobility.

United Kingdom - The travail of the United Kingdom's shipping industry has occurred over an extended period of time. Historically, the industry represented a key export industry and accounted for a substantial proportion of employment in the Glasgow (Clyde) area and also on the north-east coast. Today, employment is well under 100,000, which is only a fraction of its peak post-war level. Nothing seems to have been able to stem the tide: the first phase of mergers and consolidations gave way to the takeover of the remnants of the industry by the British government. In turn, the resulting enterprise, British Shipbuilders, has been cut back steadily to the point where it constructs ships at only a few locations and the prospects for further cutbacks are quite high.

Germany - In the German shipbuilding industry orders, production and employment have been declining almost continuously during the 1970s. Between 1974 and 1979 the German share of total world orders declined from 5.1 to 1.7 per cent or, in absolute terms, from 7.6 million to 0.5 million tons. As a result, Germany moved from the third to the sixteenth position in the rank of shipbuilding countries. Employment declined from 71,000 in the middle of 1975 to 55,000 in mid-1979; and there is an imminent threat of more job loss.

Sweden - The shipbuilding industry in Sweden was expanding its capacity through much of the period after World War II. By the early 1960s Sweden had the second largest ship production after Japan and had attained a world market share of 10 per cent.

The crisis of the industry, entailing heavy downward adjustment of capacity and employment started in 1975 - at this point 4,000 workers were idled when the Eriksberg shipyard in Gothenburg faced bankruptcy. In 1976 a cut of employment by 30 per cent from the 1974 level was targeted - to be completed by 1978. During this period 8,000 workers left the industry.

In 1978 another 20 per cent capacity reduction was mapped out. The decline was to be brought about by measures other than the shutdown of yards. Further downward adjustment was considered in 1980; this time including the possibility of closing down some operations.

Automobile Industry

The automobile industry exemplifies very vividly almost all of the essential circumstances and causes

24

which currently strike industries in most advanced Western
nations:

- market saturation (as in the United States) or a
  levelling-off of growth in demand (as in Europe);
- changes in the composition of demand, such as
  the call for smaller cars (particularly in North
  America) due to increased fuel prices;
- technical innovations in production, like the
  introduction of robots;
- organisational adjustment, as typified by the
  arrival of the standardized world car models
  based on interchangeable parts produced and
  marketed in many countries;
- the present downturn in the business cycle and
  the high sensitivity of car sales to economic
  fluctuation;
- the rapid progress by Japanese car manufacturers
  in gaining market shares both in the United
  States and in Europe.

United States - The automobile industry experienced
a dramatic loss of production, sales and employment in
1979 and 1980. This decline was unprecedented in scale.
The various causes for the crisis and for "the need for
restructuring" seem to be more striking than in the other
major auto-producing countries. There has been a cumu-
lation of down-sizing of vehicles, computerisation and
robot introduction, a fuel crisis in the recent past and
large increases in the cost of gasoline from a low level,
relocation of production facilities within the country and
to other countries, a recession starting in 1979 and a
major breakthrough of sales of Japanese cars.

The big three domestic producers of automobiles,
General Motors Corp., Ford Motor Corp. and Chrysler Corp.,
each reported large losses totalling $3.6 billion for the
first three quarters of 1980. During the third quarter of
1980, each of the companies lost around $500 million. At
the beginning of July 1980, some 268,000 workers were unemployed, 217,000 of whom were on indefinite and 51,000
workers on temporary layoff. (In contrast, during the
downturn experienced from 1973 to 1975, 213,000 workers
were out of work.) This unemployment accounted for 36 per
cent of a total labour force of 735,000 in the three
companies. The severe slump has not only affected the
automobile companies but the supplier industries as well.
Overall, an estimated 750,000 jobs have been lost in the
United States directly or indirectly related to the
drop in production of four million units from 1978.

During 1980, Chrysler announced the closing of
ten plants, resulting in a loss of 25,000 permanent jobs.
Ford announced the closing of four plants, amounting to
10,000 jobs. While General Motors announced plans to

close eight plants, it is not clear what the net job loss will be, since a number of replacement plants are being built.

United Kingdom - Automobile production in Britain was much lower towards the end of the 1970s compared with the beginning. While in 1972 nearly two million units were produced, production was less than one million in 1980. British Leyland, the national car producer in Britain, faced a dramatic reduction of sales, production and employment over the 1970s. Ten years ago the company produced more than one million cars and trucks a year, while in 1980 the figure was 587,000. During the past decade Leyland's market share for cars in Britain declined from 40 to 18 per cent. The company decided in September of 1979 to cut its work force of 165,000 by 25,000 over two years, and close 13 plants, at least partially. The future of 30 others was being reviewed. In 1981 it was reported that during the three-year period between 1978 and 1980 employment was cut by 56,000. Further sizable reductions are planned.

British Leyland sought government funding in excess of £225 million remaining from the £1 billion which already had been assigned to the firm. The plant closures were planned on the basis of performance and the existing state of modernisation. The company expected to concentrate on cars for the medium market, including models from a partnership with Honda.

Germany - The automobile industry faced a substantial slump during the recession period of 1973 to 1975 in the aftermath of the first oil shock. Overall, production declined by about 30 per cent and employment was reduced from 635,000 to 560,000 between 1973 and 1975. Volkswagen ran down its work force by about 27,000 workers, in part through natural attrition and partly through severance payment contracts and early retirement. In addition, many workers were on short-time for several months. Opel had 27,000 employees in 1975 compared to 38,000 in 1973.

Starting in the autumn of 1975 the industry experienced an unexpected boom period that ended in 1980 when the onslaught of a recession coincided with increasing gasoline prices, and sharp sales gains by the Japanese car industry generated a decrease in demand for German-built cars, particularly for the upper-medium sized models of Opel, Ford and Audi. In 1980, Japanese manufacturers sold 70 per cent more cars than the previous year in Germany, while Ford sold 19 per cent less and VW/Audi sold 13 per cent less. Opel's sales declined by 15 per cent, generating a loss of 411 million Deutschmarks. It was the company's first loss since World War II.

Whereas VW/Audi attempted to cope with the cut of production by resorting to short-time work, Ford reduced its work force by 6,000 and Opel by 7,500. Both companies offered severance pay contracts mainly to workers over 59. The main victims of job loss in the German auto industry, just as in manufacturing as a whole, have been unskilled, female, aged and foreign workers.

Italy - Fiat was struck by the recession 1974 to 1975. In 1974, it sold 12 per cent fewer automobiles than in 1973, and the work force declined by 6.5 per cent. In addition, 66,000 workers were on short time. Effective in December 1974, further measures were agreed upon between the company and the unions, comprising extended holidays. As this proved insufficient, a further agreement provided layoff of 65,000 out of 90,000 workers for 18 working days in February and March of 1975.

More recently, Fiat reported a loss of $48 million for its automobile division in the first ten months of 1980. In part this loss was a result of market slump, and in part it was due to severe labour unrest during September and October when there was almost a complete shutdown of operations. The job loss during 1980 totalled 10,000. In July 1980 the company announced a cut of production by 30 per cent in the second half of the year to keep its already large stock of unsold cars from growing to intolerable proportions.

After the disruption in the autumn and after extensive layoffs during summer 1980 (involving 78 per cent of the work force) the company reached agreement with the metal-working unions on 17 October, in which the highly contested decision to make 14,000 workers redundant was dropped. The agreement, instead, provided for reduction of the labour force by voluntary redundancies, natural attrition, early retirement, internal mobility and layoff of 23,000 workers (rotated among 30,000 instead of the full work force of 140,000 as demanded by the union) in the Turin area at any time until December 1980. Thereafter, the company in consultation with the union would decide how many of these workers will be made redundant.

II

THE CONSEQUENCES OF LARGE-SCALE
WORK FORCE DISPLACEMENT

The previous chapter has enumerated the extent of
work force displacements for a number of key industries.
Presumably, changes of the magnitude described exert
substantial impacts on the individuals and regions involved. These ramifications need to be elaborated and it
is to this task that we now turn. The order of analysis
will be from the community to the individual and from the
economic to the non-economic impacts.

AREA AND REGIONAL CONSEQUENCES

We begin this section by detailing the impact of
large-scale work force displacements for two auto-production areas in North America: the first is for the golden
horseshoe in Canada and the second, a major community in
crisis, Detroit, the automobile capital of the world.

Canada - The Canadian autombile industry is concentrated geographically with about 90 per cent of the
employment occurring in a small area stretching across
southern Ontario. In communities like Windsor, St.
Catherines and Chatham, anywhere from 40 per cent to 80
per cent of all manufacturing jobs are concentrated in the
automobile industry. Thus in Windsor, where up to 10,000
auto workers were on layoff temporarily, which represents
almost 40 per cent of workers displaced in this industry,
the consequences have been substantial. The welfare and
social case load has increased approximately 30 per cent
in a one-year period,(1) due to the indirect impact of
the auto crisis on the community.

---

1. "Auto and Crisis", Position Paper of the Canadian
Union of Auto Workers Council, 15 September 1980.

28

Detroit - The number of auto-production facilities located in Wayne County, Michigan, declined from 206 in 1951 to 145 in 1976. Since that time two more plants have been closed: the Highland Park Tractor Plant of Ford and the Dodge main plant of Chrysler in Hamatramck. Other closures have been announced: the Lynch Road Assembly Plant of Chrysler, the Outer Drive Stamping Plant of Chrysler, the Clark Avenue Engine Plant of General Motors and the Fleetwood Fisher Body Plant of General Motors. While both General Motors and Chrysler have indicated some plans for new construction, the net loss of jobs will be substantial. Chrysler employs 28,000 workers directly and accounts for the employment of 51,000 in supplier firms, all located in the immediate Detroit area.

Not surprisingly, in early 1981 the unemployment figure was 12 per cent.(2) The decline in population has also been noteworthy: from 1.5 million in 1970 to 1.1 million in 1980. Other indications of economic stress can be seen in the fact that recipients for food stamps jumped from a little over 200,000 in 1978 to 340,000 in August of 1980; and general assistance claims rose from 41,000 in 1978 to 87,000 in August of 1980.

Glasgow, United Kingdom - Seventeen of Glasgow's 20 shipyards, which employed 100,000 men and produced the Queen Mary, the Queen Elizabeth and the QE-2, have closed. So has the Singer Sewing Machine factory, which once employed nearly 20,000. Goodyear Tyre and Talbot's Linwood car plant have also ceased operations.

Ruhr, Germany - While for the country as a whole, the employment rate declined from 4.7 per cent in 1975 to 3.8 per cent in 1979, the rate remained high or increased in some labour market areas. The Ruhr district, Germany's traditional heartland of heavy industry, has become a so-called "problem" region during the 1970s. In 1975, there were only 7.2 per cent of problem areas in the Ruhr district, whereas in 1978 the amount was 44 per cent.

THE PATHOLOGY OF A COMMUNITY IN DECLINE (3)

Closer analysis of situations like those just cited reveals that a cluster of economic effects emerges over

---

2. Unemployment rates ran even higher for some auto-manufacturing centres, e.g. Flint 22 per cent; Saginaw 17 per cent; and Anderson 20 per cent; in the case of these three communities auto employment accounts for a very large fraction of manufacturing employment.
3. Some of the material in this section has been taken from an unpublished manuscript by Robert McKersie, Leonhard Greenhalgh and Todd Jick entitled: "Economic Progress and Economic Dislocation".

time. The immediate, direct effects tend to be quite visible, as the most discretionary spending income is curtailed. A multiplier effect on employment may initiate a process of slow but steady decline in the community's economic base. In addition, there may be a short-run exodus of skilled craftsmen which impedes longer-run reestablishment of local industries. Finally, in small to moderate sized communities with little economic diversity, the process of decline may be practically irreversible once it has gained momentum.

Let us briefly examine what happens to a community's economy when there is a plant closedown. The first effect to be encountered is lost retail sales due to diminished spending, altered spending patterns or, worse, the exodus of workers and their families. This reduction in the spending of former wage-earners is aggravated by the curtailment of purchases of local goods and services by the closed down plant. The combined effect of the loss of these two sources of local purchases is the loss of secondary jobs in the community, including trade, construction, finance, transportation and public service. When the local economy establishes a new equilibrium, the multiplier effect will probably be seen to have taken its toll of two to three times the employees and payroll directly involved in the plant that has closed.

There are further costs that should be counted in the community-impact statement. For instance, there should be expected a direct loss in local taxes as people move on and property values decline. Further tax losses would be incurred in cases where it is necessary to use tax breaks to attract replacement industry, in addition to the expenditure of tax revenues as direct costs of "recruiting" new plants.

In addition to the economic impact, a plant closure or other work force upheaval can seriously impair the quality of life in a community. First, it is evident that individuals experiencing job loss withdraw from community life. Thus stricken communities are likely to experience diminished church attendance and generally reduced participation in social organisations. This withdrawal dampens the community's vitality, weakens the bonds that form the social fabric of the community, and consequently creates a gloomy climate that encourages out-migration, thus exacerbating the community's morbidity.

The manifestations of social withdrawal explained above are only the milder symptoms. Economic decline is also associated with social deviancy - in other words, the stricken community is likely to be that much more of a "jungle" than the healthy community, since one reaction to job loss is anomie. For instance, Harvey Brenner found that when the unemployment rate rises, so do the

rates of homicide and state prison admissions. Furthermore, there is an increase in the rate of suicide, the
ultimate withdrawal from society.(4)

PATTERNS OF COMMUNITY RESPONSE

The single most important variable explaining the impact of work force displacement on a community is the
proportion of the community's workers involved in the
primary cutbacks. We have identified a number of instances
where job loss can be taken "in stride" by a community,
precisely because the changes could be "digested". In a
study of three plant shutdowns in upstate New York, the
system-wide impacts two years later were negligible and in
the case of one community the economic health was actually
better as a result of the challenge posed by the plant
shutdown. While unemployment rates had risen to over
10 per cent immediately after the shutdown, over the ensuing years the community "healed" itself and any permanent
damage to the economic system could not be detected.(5)

A second factor that explains the severity of long-
term consequences relates to the economic specialisation
of the region. Where one-industry towns exist, like Corby,
England, or Detroit, Michigan, then the consequences are
bound to be substantial. However, in situations where the
workers displaced from one industry can move, within the
commuting area of the labour market, to the openings in
other industries, then the long-term consequences are
minimized. For example, in the case of Japan, it has been
possible for excess workers in the steel industry to take
up employment in the automobile industry. In this respect,
it would appear that Japan and (to some extent) Germany
today are well situated because of the large diversified
industrial areas that exist in these countries. By contrast, the United States, with its Detroit automobile
concentration, Youngstown steel concentration, and Akron
rubber concentration, has encountered structural unemployment because the concentrations of displaced workers are
not able to shift to other industries in the local labour
markets - either because other industries do not exist, or
if they do, because their employment fluctuates in synchronisation with the basic industries due to their relationship as suppliers and contractors.

---

4. M.H. Brenner, Estimating the Social Costs of
National Economic Policy: Implications for Mental and
Physical Health and Criminal Aggression. A study prepared
for the Joint Economic Committee, US Congress, USGPO,
Washington, 1976.
5. Robert Aronson and Robert McKersie, "Economic
Consequences of Plant Shutdowns in New York State", May
1980 (unpublished).

IMPACT OF JOB LOSS FOR THE INDIVIDUALS INVOLVED

Aside from the aggregate effects described above, job loss for the individuals involved represents a very personal event and even where the overall statistics might not indicate any difficulties, certainly for the individuals involved severe transitional consequences are likely to be experienced. We will consider these impacts both with respect to the economic and non-economic dimensions.

Economic impact on individuals – The most concrete and perhaps the most visible impact of job loss is in the economic sphere. The severity of income loss for the individuals affected varies with many factors. The state of the labour market (the number of jobs available), the personal characteristics of the individual (age, sex and experience) and the mobility of the individual all have a direct bearing on whether the person suffers any economic hardship as a result of job loss. Even controlling for some of the variables just mentioned, the range of economic experience can be quite wide. At one extreme are individuals who ultimately do better as a result of change, usually not more than 10 per cent of the terminated population. Such individuals "land on their feet" with better jobs than they had before the shutdown. At the other end of the spectrum is a group that suffers long-term unemployment and may even end up on welfare. This is a group for whom job loss can be catastrophic, leading to loss of all savings, forced sale of capital goods such as automobiles and housing, and a "nose dive into poverty".

The best guess as to the typical economic impact of job loss is that it costs the individual something in excess of $21,000 in the United States.(6) A large part of this sum is due to lower earnings brought about by the fact that the subsequent job does not pay as well as the job which was lost. Another way of saying the same thing is that the worker takes a capital loss because the human capital that had been developed within the particular situation cannot be marketed for the same value. Beyond losses in human capital, other losses come in the form of moving household goods, out-of-pocket costs for travel to search for new employment, decline in the capital value of homes and the like.

The varying economic consequences can be illustrated from three studies from the United States, the United Kingdom and Japan.

United States – Two years after the shutdown of three plants in upstate New York, researchers found the

6. Louis Jacobson and Janet Thomasen, Earnings Loss Due to Displacement, Public Research Institute, Arlington, Virginia, July 1979.

following: three quarters of the workers had found new
jobs; 14 per cent had left the labour market; and 10 per
cent were unemployed. For those finding new jobs the decline in earnings was substantial and about one fifth
reported a major reduction in family income. This reflected the fact that in about 25 per cent of the cases
other members of the household entered the labour market
after the layoff of the primary breadwinner.(7)

United Kingdom - Based on a summary of redundancy
studies prepared for the United Kingdom's Department of
Employment, the following emerged. Half of the displacees
experienced periods of unemployment in excess of ten weeks.
Individuals who seemed to be primarily in this category
were older and unskilled. Anywhere from 2 per cent to
10 per cent left the labour force, with women especially
following this route. Geographical mobility ranged from
3 per cent to about 20 per cent.(8)

Japan - Some 2,000 Japanese workers, who had been
displaced from the shipbuilding industry in Nagasaki, were
surveyed in February of 1980. Based on 848 returns the
following major points emerged from the survey. A total
of 287 fell in the age group 50 to 59. Whereas only 24
workers had been temporary employees previously, 105 fell
into this category with their new employment. Over 250
individuals had experienced unemployment in excess of one
year. About 10 per cent of the total were still unemployed at the time of the survey. Monthly earnings
decreased for 478 and only increased for 140 individuals.
Regarding the nature of employment, 303 said that it had
become more unstable, while 139 said it had become more
stable. From the cross-tabulations it is clear that adverse consequences affected older workers and women
workers much more frequently than their counterparts.(9)

Impact on the quality of life - Although job loss
has traditionally been viewed as an economic phenomenon,
a growing body of literature has been documenting its
ripple effects throughout the affected individual's life-
space.

The psychological response of the individual to job
loss ranges over a wide spectrum. Certain individuals
who thrive on change respond to the challenge of job loss
quite effectively and their emotional well-being may
actually improve as a result of the event. At the other
extreme we find individuals who never recover from the

_____

7. Robert Aronson and Robert McKersie, op. cit.
8. Unpublished study.
9. A Survey of Displaced Workers from the Shipbuilding Industry by the Employment Creation Committee of
Nagasaki Prefecture, March 1980.

trauma of job loss. Some authors have taken advantage of
what is already known about the grief reaction in explainin
the reaction of the individual to job loss. Depending on
the level of ego involvement in the job, job loss may be
seen as akin to any type of major loss, such as death of a
loved one, loss of an arm or leg, or the destruction of
one's home as a result of a natural disaster.   Some individuals can quickly re-establish themselves and develop a
new platform on which to continue living;   others are never
able to cope and remain emotionally impaired the rest of
their lives

It is further known that, by and large, men appear to
have more difficulty in handling the psychological consequences of job loss than do women. This is probably due
to the fact that holding a job is more central to the self-
concept of men than it is for women (at least at the
present time). It may also be that the economic loss will
generally be greater for men and thus the psychological
consequences greater. One interesting consequence of the
increasing participation of women in the work force and
the possible liberation of men to adopt non-remunerative
activities of caring for the children and managing the
household is that the consequences of job loss may lessen
for men and increase for women.

In addition, the intensity of the emotional reaction
to job loss appears to be greater for white-collar than
blue-collar workers. White-collar workers typically
assume, or may even be assured by management, that they
enjoy job security - here the reality of displacement
comes as a severe shock.

The psychological reaction to job loss is not mono-
lithic; it changes over time. In fact, almost all individuals pass through several stages of emotional reaction.
The first stage is that of denial: when news is un-
believable, the only way to handle the situation is to
suppress the event. This period of defensive shock is
quite understandable because all signals of the employment
relationship had pointed towards security and continuity,
and the announcement that the organisation is going to be
terminated hits most people as something they cannot
reconcile with their assumptions. In most organisations,
as years of service increase, employees feel more and more
secure. Seniority counts for something in terms of fringe
benefits, and if temporary layoffs followed by recalls
occur, then seniority is often used as the allocation
device. Then, too, the employer most likely cultivates
the impression of continuity as a way of maintaining an
intact work force.

The employment relationship must be seen as akin to
any social relationship. During the period the parties
are in accord, considerable stability and reinforcement
takes place. However, as the relationship is breaking

up, considerable bitterness and destructive behaviour can take place. This is what social scientists call "end game" behaviour. If the employer has indicated that the business is going to be terminated in the near future, the counter-reaction may well be: "Why shouldn't I 'jump ship' as soon as possible and find other employment; why shouldn't I use up all my sick leave; or why shouldn't I give just minimal effort while I am looking for employment else-where?"

THE POLITICAL IMPACT

By far the most important dimension of large-scale work force displacements is political. Given the severity, both qualitatively and quantitatively, of displacements, it is not surprising that substantial worker protest has developed during the last decade. During the late 1960s and the first half of the 1970s, several hundred factory occupations occurred in France and a similar number in the United Kingdom - in the case of the latter country it was estimated that 150,000 workers participated in these protests against decisions to close plants and cut back employment.(10)

While the response to displacement in the form of protest and group action has characterised Europe more than other regions, even in Japan, where the reaction to change has been reasonably accommodating, there have been marches. On the Canadian scene, there is the picture of increasing resistance to cutbacks and in several instances workers have occupied plants as protest to the cutbacks.

But not all massive displacements result in the social and political reaction just described. For example, there are industries that have experienced rapid rundown of employment and yet there has not been the controversy and the attention shown that is currently the case. For example, in the United States during the 1950s and 1960s the textile industry left New England, thereby temporarily stranding over 100,000 workers. Between 1969 and 1971, due to massive cutbacks in defence spending and shifts in priorities, the Boeing Corporation laid off 70,000 workers out of a total employment of 110,000. Many of these workers had been employed in the north-west region of the United States. In the case of United Kingdom textiles between 1951 and 1966, employment dropped from 360,000 to

---

10. Tom Clarke, "Redundancy, Worker Resistance and the Community" in Gary Craig, et al., Jobs and Community Action, Routledge and Kegan Paul, London, 1979.

145,000 as part of a conscious programme to scale down the size of the industry and to upgrade its technology.(11)

Certainly, it must be recognised that the scale effect mentioned earlier is a critical factor in explaining the reaction of the community and, indeed, the country to economic change. It is one thing for a series of plants producing electronic products, none of them employing more than 1,000 people, to be shut down. Thus, when RCA dropped its employment from 21,000 to slightly over 7,000 between 1969 and 1979, the country was aware that it was losing a good part of its electronics industry but there was not the national concern that is currently the case. In contrast, when several automobile companies lay off over 200,000 workers (as in the United States) with much of this concentrated in a few labour market areas, the impact is bound to be different, and certainly perceived in drastically different terms.

Another explanation is that "times have changed" and workers and their union representatives are not willing to accept economic change and the ensuing displacement as the "breaks of the game". Without developing an elaborate explanation, it appears that many industrialised societies have become much more societies of protest and are fighting for vested interests. Women in the labour market are asserting their rights. For example, many of the workers who were displaced from textiles both in New England and the United Kingdom were women, and during the 1950s and 1960s they accepted these changes as "inevitable". It is unlikely, if changes of these magnitudes occur again, that the response on the part of the workers involved would be as fatalistic.

---

11. Caroline Miles, Lancashire Textiles, Cambridge University Press, 1968.

III

THE NATURE OF THE ECONOMIC CHANGES TAKING PLACE

THE CHALLENGE AT PRESENT: TOWARDS A
NEW DIVISION OF LABOUR IN THE WORLD ECONOMY

Economic development does not always take place smoothly, but tends to possess a cyclical dynamic. These cycles frequently produce waves of worker displacement and dislocation. Looking at periods of intensive structural change in the past we notice the waves of rationalisation in the United States and Europe during the 1920s and the wave of mechanisation and automation during the 1950s and early 1960s. Accompanying these periods of intense technological innovation, there were phases of accelerated sectoral changes in the economy, like the decline of the primary industries (agriculture and mining) and decline and expansion within various industrial sectors.

Another cycle of major restructuring set in during the 1970s; it has, by now, generated a new economic and social environment. This time, the wave of change appears to involve nothing less than a sweeping re-division of labour on a world-wide scale for substantial segments of industrial production.

Major shifts of production have occurred across the core industrial countries - the United States and Europe have lost competitive power and market shares to Japan - but more importantly, new countries have built up considerable industrial production capacity and have entered into competition with virtually all of the established industrial nations. Typically, the newcomers have distinctive advantages, such as more recent and, therefore, more modern production plant and equipment (often imported from the advanced countries), low wage cost, limited or weak trade unions, few or low labour standards and environmental protection and low cost energy and raw materials.

Erosion of competitiveness of the core industrial
countries, as could be expected, came first in industries
of high labour intensity and large components of low-
skilled workers, such as in textiles, clothing, electrical
and optical goods. Subsequently, a growing challenge came
from such countries as South Korea, Taiwan, Malaysia,
Brazil and Mexico in fields with more sophisticated,
capital-intensive technology, like shipbuilding, iron and
steel, automobiles, engineering and electronics. And a
number of further countries now appear to be at the door-
step of large-scale manufacturing and capable of entering
world markets.

The advances made by newly industrialised countries
in many areas of industrial products has stepped up
competition for mass products and has prompted some of
the old established nations to emphasize the production
of more specialised, high technology goods to compensate
for some of the losses in mass production. Others, rather
than following the forward strategy of innovation and
modernisation, have taken a rather defensive, protectionist posture with the effect that structural adjustment has
been delayed.

The move towards a new division of labour on a world-
wide scale may have originated in the large divergence of
production costs, notably labour costs, between the old
and the new industrial countries, and by the efforts of
many of the core industrial countries to expand, through
exports, their markets for consumer and investment goods.
While these conditions prevailed in the 1960s, further
events occurred during the 1970s, accelerating the pace of
restructuring. Most important among them were:

- the breakdown of the monetary order of fixed
  exchange rates in 1973, triggering a series of
  devaluations and revaluations of national
  currencies and producing a shift in the
  competitiveness of many products in international markets;
- rapid increases in the price of energy and
  raw materials, altering the terms of trade
  across countries and within countries (such
  as the shift of manufacturing from the "frost
  belt" to the "sun belt" in the United States).

Yet, it seems doubtful whether the emerging shifts
in the international division of labour as such could
have generated the present critical employment situation
in many established Western industrial nations had they
not been compounded or accelerated by other developments.

There have been a number of overriding developments
during the 1970s that tended to aggravate the employment
effects emanating from structural shifts:

- The globalisation of markets. It is fashionable
  to talk about the world car with components
  produced in a variety of countries depending
  upon respective cost advantages. This de-
  integration of production is illustrated by the
  exporting of logs to Japan by large United States
  lumber companies - as a result 10,000 workers
  have been displaced from lumber-processing
  and related jobs.
- The synchronisation of business cycles and
  cycles of product innovation. Both have
  heightened the vulnerability of national economies to external pressures as changes are not
  dispersed but happen everywhere at the same
  time.
- Increased speed of structural adjustment due
  to higher rates of innovation and development
  of product and process as well as better
  systems of communication and transportation.(1)
- Multinational firms with a world view have
  accelerated the shift process as they have redeployed assets across national boundaries.
- Inflationary pressures and particularly high
  interest rates have driven many businesses to
  the point of bankruptcy as costs have increased
  while weak product markets have made it im-
  possible to pass on the higher costs to the
  customers.
- The restrictive economic and fiscal policies
  followed by governments to counter inflation
  have contributed to low rates of economic
  growth.
- The shrinkage of the volume of world trade
  during the present recession.

These factors, taken together, have not only extended the scale of economic contraction and job loss,
but have also affected the damage or social cost of
worker displacement. They have lessened the chances
that workers displaced by structural adjustment will find
new jobs. Thus, in the face of declining economic growth
rates and rising unemployment levels, there has been a

1. This point can be illustrated by the rapid advancement of micro-electronics. It appears as if never
before in industrial history has a major new technology
arrived and spread as precipitously as the micro-
processor. Developed in 1969 by the American firm Intel,
it took the micro-processor merely six years to pass
through three generations of development. The impact of
the diffusion of this innovation has been tremendous. For
example, the watch industry in West Germany, located in
parts of the state of Baden-Württemberg (representing a
small fraction of the larger German electronics sector of
about one million employment), lost every second job between 1970 and 1975 following the breakthrough of electronics in this industry).

lowering of the readiness of workers to accept structural changes and mobility. In short, it is the coincidence of the new division of labour and of low economic growth levels which characterises the current unfavourable environment.

TYPES OF CAPITAL SHIFTS

Within the ongoing process of internationalisation of production and commerce, economic restructuring takes various forms. There are various ways to think about the subject of investment and disinvestment. We use a distinction that is most relevant for understanding the impact of economic change on employment. Basically, we can differentiate the deployment of capital to change products and processes within existing industries (re-investment) from the shift of capital from the declining to the growing industries (disinvestment plus new investment).

The first form of structural adjustment can be called internal and is handled within a firm or plant by introducing new products and technology or by improving the utilisation of plant equipment and human resources. Restructuring may also happen through reallocation external to particular firms, i.e. by the decline of industries and firms and the growth of others and by a similar external, inter-firm reallocation of labour. Policy approaches in this case are directed towards encouraging and easing the reallocation of the resources affected. The distinction between these two categories of structural change may be blurred if adjustment comes about through mergers of firms, product diversification and other forms of industry reorganisation. A good illustration of this mixture can be seen in the experience of the food retailing industry in the United States, which has gone through a number of dramatic changes wherein the large supermarkets have automated while many of the independent supermarkets have captured larger shares of the business in the same geographical areas.

Internal restructuring has gained in importance relative to external adjustment especially in Europe. In part this evolution is due to the process of growing concentration of industry, but also to the increased search for job security, employment stabilisation and other elements of fixed costs of labour at the firm or plant level. Nevertheless, there remain important sectors in national economies where structural adjustment proceeds in an external fashion - by the contraction and expansion of firms and industries. Thus, the current depressed industries with large-scale loss of jobs, like shipbuilding, textiles and automobiles, show relatively low overall potential of internal transfer of resources to new and different product categories; therefore, the changes are bound to lower their employment levels substantially.

Within the steel industry, there have been some attempts to widen the scope for internal transfer of production capacity, as, for example, through the expansion of steel companies in the engineering and metal-working fields. Similarly, big automobile companies have made efforts in recent years to diversify their range of products so as to reduce the risk from sudden decline of monostructured production. All of these are examples of internal restructuring. Nevertheless, most of the adjustment occurring in the steel and auto industries in most countries must be characterised as external.

Certainly it is the case that in many situations a combination of both internal and external restructuring strategies is underway. For example, in the United States, the automobile industry appears to be going through a sharp downward shift in demand for workers (external restructuring) at the same time that the type of employment required due to the new technology is also changing (internal restructuring). The United States rubber industry also vividly illustrates the simultaneous evolution of both internal and external developments. With respect to internal restructuring we would mention the shifts to new technology in the production of radial tyres; the shift to new methods of compensation (the abandonment of piece-work in favour of day-work) and a number of other changes that have moved the industry to a continuous shift operation and a more full utilisation of plant and equipment. On the other hand, the fall-off in demand and the difficulty that some companies such as Firestone have experienced must be seen as part of an external restructuring development. Also, the policy of a number of companies to operate on a non-union basis and to open plants in areas where it is feasible to remain non-union is a strategy that provokes severe employment consequences for established manufacturing centres. But it is hard to classify this as either internal or external. To grasp the dimensions of this development, the rubber industry (which just ten years ago was almost 100 per cent organised) has now moved to a point where from 20 per cent to 30 per cent of its production workers are not unionised.

SYSTEMATIC COMPARISON OF EXTERNAL VERSUS
INTERNAL RESTRUCTURING ACTIVITIES

The following figure compares in summary form the two methods of restructuring that we have been presenting:

	External Restructuring	Internal Restructuring
Nature of the change	Drop in demand and a shift of capital and labour from the declining to the expanding industries	Change in products and technology and internal reallocation of the work force
Pace of the change	Reasonably rapid	May be implemented more slowly
Geographical implications	New locations	Usually same locations
Source of financial assistance	Often outside sources, especially government	May be generated from working capital or banks

Nature of the change - Several industries have been forced into external restructuring on a world-wide basis since they have experienced a substantial fall in demand, for example shipbuilding and steel. In other situations the fall-off in demand may affect a given industry in some countries more than in others (for example the automobile industry). In other instances, the restructuring may have been triggered as a result of shifts in demand across competing products. For example, when the United Kingdom entered the Common Market, a shift in refining sugar to the "beet" method meant that Tate and Lyle, which had been in sugar production by the "cane" method had to institute substantial cutbacks in a number of its refineries.

By contrast, internal restructuring describes an upgrading of facilities, a movement to new technology and a modernisation of operations. This has been happening on a world-wide basis in the textile industry for some time. Other important examples of internal restructuring can be seen in the shift to the production of radial tyres with a different technology in the rubber industry, as well as the introduction of robots in the automobile industry.

Pace of the change - By its very nature external restructuring usually comes on an industry quickly and there are few ways available to slow down the pace of change. If demand falls off, then there is little that can be done to forestall the employment consequences. But with internal restructuring, the life of old equipment can be prolonged and the improvement in operations can be planned over several years. This is especially true of programmes to lower costs and to improve productivity through the introduction of various labour-saving

devices. It is also the case in terms of shifting production to more modern facilities. For example, a number of
tobacco companies in the United States have been moving
production away from old factories in urban areas to modern
one-storey factories in rural areas where space is much
more available to lay out the modern technology.

Geographical implications - Often, external restructuring means a geographical shift in the concentration
of employment, because typically the growing industries
are not located in the same areas as the declining industries. By contrast, with the development of modern facilities, the introduction of new technology can take place in
the same labour market areas as the old facilities. For
example, General Motors has agreed to construct most of
its new plants in existing labour markets.

Government assistance - Outside financial assistance,
especially from the government, is much more likely to be
involved in external than in internal restructuring. A
variety of government programmes to assist developing
industries, that is picking and assiting the "winners",
occurs in almost all industrialised countries.

By contrast, internal restructuring is less likely
to involve governmental help and usually, if outside
financial assistance is involved, it comes from the banks.
For example, Toyo Kogyo, producer of Mazdas, faced a
severe crisis in 1974 when its Wankel-powered Mazdas
"flopped" in the market due to their high gasoline con-
sumption. In the face of this financial problem, one of
the leading banks, Sumitomo, lent a substantial sum of
money (30 per cent of the company's debt) and as a result
the company was able to re-tool and get back on its feet.

A similar experience occurred in Germany about the
same time. The Volkswagen Company faced a rapidly de-
teriorating economic situation in 1974 and 1975, and (at
its low point), in the spring of 1975, the Company was
quickly approaching insolvency. Although the federal and
state governments were the largest among VW's shareholders,
both levels of government resisted calls by management
and labour representatives to help end the financial
crisis. Rather, government insisted upon a free-enterprise
solution.

Occasionally governments do provide financial assistance for internal restructuring. During the 1960s,
for example, the German government financially aided the
restructuring of the coalmining industry, and, in the
1970s, in the German steel industry the government yielded
to requests for public aid for modernisation and adjustment programmes. The case in point concerns the
Roechling-Burback Company and Neunkircher Eisenwerke, two
of the largest steel producers in the Saar district and
of vital significance for the employment of this depressed

region.(2) The two companies were hit exceptionally hard
by the steel crisis. In contrast to other German steel
companies which had altered their production programme in
favour of quality and special steel products, the Saar
companies still concentrated on basic steel and, in this
field, faced strong competition from Italian steel plants.
In addition, the geographical location of the Saar mills
relative to users and raw materials supplies was unfavourable, the technology used was partly out-dated, and
finally, work rules made changes in production more difficult.

In 1978, after the two companies were taken over by
the Luxembourg-based ARBED S.A. group, the two companies
came forward with a five-year modernisation and rationalisation programme aimed at regaining profitability of the
operations and enhancing job security, but only after a
planned reduction of employment by 8,800. The ARBED
group did not see itself in a position to finance the restructuring scheme from its own resources. Therefore, the
federal government and the state government, in light of
the strategic importance of the two companies for the
regional labour market, stepped in to provide (to both
companies) a loan guarantee of 900 million Deutschmarks
paid in five instalments over the five-year implementation
period of the plan. The public aid provided investment
for modern plant and equipment and enabled the firms to
stretch the run-down of the work force over a longer
period of time.

One conclusion that can be drawn from these cases is
that governmental subsidies are more likely the larger
the scale and the more devastating the prospective dislocation of employment for an area or region.

_____

    2. Autorengemeinschaft, Sozialpolitik in der Eisen-
und Stahl-industrie, Bund Verlag, Köln, 1979.

IV

STRATEGIC RESPONSES TO ECONOMIC RESTRUCTURING

In this chapter we make the transition from the background analysis of the nature and extent of economic restructuring to a discussion of various activities for dealing with the employment dislocations that are involved: either actual or potential.

To anticipate the development of thinking in this chapter, we will examine a spectrum of strategies ranging from purely remedial efforts that only deal with the consequences of economic change to programmes that are purely preventive, that is, they deal with the prospect of economic dislocation by preventing it from happening. In between are various approaches that can be labelled integrative, wherein both the capital and labour considerations are balanced to the greatest extent possible. Several examples will be given of integrative approaches across a number of countries.

THE HISTORICAL EVOLUTION OF STRATEGIES, POLICIES AND MEASURES

The past twenty years have been marked by an extensive and rapid development of approaches towards structural adjustment. This expansion is reflected in the heavily increasing public outlays for adjustment as well as in the increased institutional network operating at the firm level as well as in the governmental area on local, regional, national and international levels.

Prior to World War II several countries had developed, although in a more rudimentary form, policies of unemployment insurance, employment exchange and public relief work. After World War II regional and industrial policies were initiated, based primarily on investment premiums and subsidies for depressed areas and for shrinking industries.

45

The 1960s were marked by the spread of public policies for training and retraining and other forms of promotion of worker mobility; through the 1970s, the emphasis in labour market policies was increasingly directed towards job maintenance and job creation in private industry through public subsidisation of wage costs. These schemes may be regarded as a response to the inadequacy of aggregate demand management policies to deal with the stagflation problem (1) and also to the growing divergence of economic development and unemployment across and within national economies throughout the 1970s. In view of this divergence it is not surprising that the labour market policies of the 1970s evidence a tendency towards more selective, categorial and targeted application for particular industries, geographical areas and labour force groups.

At the same time higher aggregate rates of unemployment and higher differentiation of unemployment were answered by more job protection and redundancy compensation through law and collective agreements. During the second half of the 1970s, as it turned out, the employment problems were not merely cyclical but of more of a structural nature emanating from a worldwide re-division of labour. Consequently, the responses shifted from temporary schemes of public assistance to more permanent and more preventive type approaches. In the face of very small or negative economic growth rates and shrinking world trade, competition on both domestic and international markets grew harsher. In this situation governments have stepped in either to shield their most affected industries from a rapid loss of output and employment (the protectionist stance) or, to the contrary, they have accepted the challenge from intense competition by accelerating the pace of structural conversion towards more competitive products and processes (the aggressive stance).

Today, practically all of the Western industrialised nations are not merely confronted with internal conflicts between different goals, as between economic progress and economic and social security, but they are also facing heightened expectations, minimum standards or guidelines set by law, agreement or public opinion setting the limits of acceptability for the resolution of these conflicts. Values and sentiments have changed in society, placing much greater emphasis on (or taking much more for granted) individual rights to employment or even claims to a particular job.

---

1. Gösta Rehn, "Recent Trends in Western Economics: Needs and Methods for Further Development of Manpower Policy", in: Re-examining European Manpower Policies, A Special Report for the National Commission for Manpower Policy, Special Report No. 10, Washington, August 1976.

In addition, standards for the quality of work and employment have risen. Structural change, according to these, must not lead to jobs that have lower pay, require less skill, require more commuting, have worse working conditions. These standards and expectations channel and constrain the paths for structural adjustment. While they imply social progress and, thus, should not be relaxed without necessity, they also make it more difficult to conceive of and find ways out of impending employment problems.

COMPETING PHILOSOPHICAL APPROACHES

The following figure summarises the extreme strategies:

SPECTRUM OF STRATEGIES FOR DEALING WITH THE EMPLOYMENT CONSEQUENCES OF ECONOMIC RESTRUCTURING

Overal strategy	Laissez-faire	Preventive
Economic change	Uninhibited	Controlled or stopped
Employment consequences	Remedial	Averted
Role of government	Minimal	Major

On the one hand, there is the laissez-faire approach embodying the assumption that people can take care of themselves and the best course to follow is to allow economic change to take place in an uninhibited fashion and to let solutions emerge through the interplay of free market forces. The principle of this approach is: "Let industry have its natural course". This laissez-faire posture usually starts from the belief that a free enterprise system and reliance on market forces will produce the most efficient outcome of the process of structural adjustment. Any interference with competitive forces and the free mobility of capital and labour in line with market forces will inevitably impair an optimal resource allocation and prevent the best solution from coming about.

In the laissez-faire approach jobs are not protected and the impact of the change may not even be cushioned for the workers involved. Historically, this approach characterised the early phases of the industrial revolution, and of the countries in our study probably the

United States comes closest to this approach. However, in the United States there has been growing concern for the impact of the change, and some of the consequences may be dealt with in <u>remedial</u> fashion. The term "remedial" means that the decision to undertake restructuring has been made and the objective of the policies is to cushion the impact of the dislocation for the workers, firms and communities involved.

The other distinct philosophy is <u>protective</u>, specifically of the workers involved. It starts from the premise that workers affected by economic change are impacted adversely through "no fault of their own". It points to the hardship and the difficulties encountered by the workers who bear the brunt of change, and the emphasis is on policy approaches towards <u>averting</u> economic dislocation. In the extreme, it means that economic changes do not take place because the costs for individuals potentially involved would be higher than the gains to the economy, given various assumptions and orientations to the trade-offs involved between economic and worker security.

THE LAISSEZ-FAIRE APPROACH IN PRACTICE

It is not necessary to spend much time illustrating the <u>laissez-faire</u> approach since it is against this backdrop that most of the experience of industrialised countries has evolved. Indeed, the move towards preventive programmes has sprung out of the harshness of economic change and the painful experience of people caught in the structural unemployment that has characterised many periods of the industrial revolution.

One example of an industry that has experienced a series of major economic changes without extensive government involvement is the textile industry in the United States. One period of change involved the movement of most manufacturing activity from New England to the South during the 1940s and 1950s. More recently the industry has increased productivity with new mechanisation. About the only government connection with these change-overs has been through the operation of the unemployment insurance system.

PREVENTIVE APPROACHES

As the preceding section on the historical evolution of strategies indicated, the significant trend of the past twenty years has been a movement towards more preventive measures for dealing with economic dislocation. The

48

driving force has come from the expectations and sense of
entitlement to employment continuity on the part of the
working population.

There are several considerations under which preventive measures have been justified. One is the idea of
allowing enterprises to retain their incumbent labour
force (rather than redeploying workers through reduction
and recommitment of employment). The retention of the experienced work force makes sense economically where skills
are specific to particular jobs or sets of jobs so that new
human capital investment would have to be made in the case
of new recruits. A second consideration in favour of
employment maintenance relates to the substantial and well-
known monetary and social costs of unemployment which
could be avoided by keeping surplus workers on the payroll
for some time. Thus, it has been emphasized that in some
countries the costs accruing to the public treasuries
from income maintenance to an unemployed worker may be
nearly as high or higher than the cost of subsidizing
continued employment. Therefore, given the large returns
from any transfer from unemployment to employment, it is
understandable that governments have been keen to apply
such measures.

Perhaps the pendulum has reached its limit in emphasizing the costs of change (and we will be talking about
a better balance in the latter sections of Chapter IV
that deal with integrative approaches to restructuring);
nevertheless, it is important to summarise the various
categories into which preventive programmes fall.

Conceptually, one can distinguish three approaches
to the objective of preventing dislocation. First, the
firm or industry can be shielded from the pressures of
change by some type of protectionist measures. Thus, the
employment disruptions never occur because the product
market has been stabilized. Second, the firm that is
facing the prospect of demise with all the attendant disruption can be "bailed out" by government. The use of
the term "bail out" suggests that the object of the aid
is to avoid the permanent layoff of the workers rather
than to foster restructuring and a transition to more
viable arrangements. Finally, we come to measures that
can be termed employment stabilisation. These programmes
consist of temporary assistance to firms to provide continuity of employment even though jobs are being eliminated and economic restructuring is taking place.

It should be clear that as we consider these three
approaches, we will be moving from examples that are
essentially negative to those that are primarily positive
examples of adjustment measures.

Trade protection - One approach is to turn away
from an international economy and resume a more national

49

orientation by erecting barriers to trade and establishing local content rules: "Let goods be homespun", as
Keynes said. This protectionist approach carries many
problems and risks. Outputs of protected national industries are the inputs to other national industries, which
dislike buying from high-cost national suppliers and are
likely to turn to cheaper imported products. Thus, either
the protection is extended to become effective or the
problem of non-competitive costs is merely shifted to
another industry.

Similarly, the introduction of protectionism in one
country is likely to lead to similar measures in other
countries. There are links, for example, between the
economic and financial capacity of developing countries
and the economic growth of the developed countries. If
the developing countries cannot expand their exports
because of trade barriers errected in the advanced
countries, they must cut down on imports, which, in consequence, will lead to lower economic activity in the
export-oriented economies.

Rescue operations – A second strategy which engenders
great dangers is one of un-coordinated public subsidisation of troubled industries in the hope that they will
gain a competitive edge over industries in the other
countries. This subsidisation of troubled industries has
occurred in a number of countries, but no doubt some of
the best known examples have occurred in the United
Kingdom. The programmes have followed several forms. The
most highly publicised is the bail-out, wherein the
troubled company or industry is rescued either through
nationalisation or a large loan from the National Enterprise Board. The United Kingdom is not alone and the
United States has underway a bail-out programme for
Chrysler; and other examples can be found in the
Scandinavian and Mediterranean countries.

Usually, these programmes are justified by some type
of "balance sheet" analysis that shows that the governmental treasury will be better off by putting funds into
the company to save the jobs, rather than allowing the lay
offs to take place with the concomitant necessity of
financing a series of unemployment and welfare contributions.

Despite some passionate political feeling and the
balance sheet work by economists, most evaluations have
concluded that rescue operations cannot be justified on
an economic basis. It has been noted by a number of
analysts that programmes that start out as short-run
solutions to avoid large employment disruptions are difficult to abandon over the long run. For example,
Australia in the mid-1970s instituted a series of support
programmes for textiles, clothing and footwear, and
passenger motor vehicles in order to avoid large-scale

displacements. The government has been forced to continue these programmes and has given a commitment that
they will be maintained until at least 1988.

Employment stabilisation - The general aim of public
schemes for stabilising employment is to provide temporary
assistance (subsidies, allowances, etc.) to enterprises
in order to maintain jobs or employment in periods of
reduced manpower need. As a rule, it is assumed that unemployment of surplus workers is avoided by keeping them
on the payroll.

Most of the schemes in operation were developed or
amended in response to increased economic fluctuations of
aggregate demand during the 1970s. They were designed to
help private employers save labour costs during economic
downturns for workers who were not fully utilized. Some
schemes are also considered to bridge the period of
reduced labour requirements during structural conversion
or reorganisation of the firm. Thus, being clearly con-
ceived of as temporary measures, these schemes are to be
distinguished from more long-term public subsidies to
wages, output or capital or the takeover of enterprises
or industries by the government.

Though it is clear that these measures are not
primarily used to extend the life of permanently declining
or uncompetitive firms or industries, they still have
some significance as measures for avoiding major employment dislocation. From an ex ante viewpoint, one does
not always know whether a fall in demand signals a
temporary or permanent decline. Therefore, it makes
sense in this case to apply stabilisation policies until
the nature of the decline becomes more apparent. Only if
the measures are applied more permanently is there a
major risk that they impede structural adjustment. The
temporary maintenance aid to the incumbent work force may,
furthermore, be used to reduce work force reduction
through means other than lay-offs.

Second, if a decision is made to attempt to save the
enterprise through restructuring, modernisation or product
change, employment maintenance schemes may be of valuable
assistance to handle the transitional phase of increased
costs. The overall value may be enhanced if the period of
idleness is used for efforts to train the under-utilised
work force. For, even if it turns out that despite the
temporary maintenance the redundancy of workers cannot
be avoided, the intermediary training may still enhance
the chances of the displaced workers to find alternative
employment.

Finally, public support may be targeted to maintain
the employment of particular groups of workers; for
example, of those whose risk of not being re-employed is
especially high. Thus, these schemes may be a meaningful

51

response to the increased concentration of unemployment (so-called structuralisation of unemployment and increasing labour market segmentation) among certain categories of labour (older workers, women and minorities).

The measures used to maintain jobs or employment are of different types:(2)

- Direct subsidies to wages.
- Subsidies to short-time work programmes.
- Subsidies to production, inventories or goods purchase in the hope that employment maintenance effects will arise.

1. Direct wage subsidies - In Japan, the employment subsidy programme has to be seen in relation to the system of lifetime employment commitment of large parts of the work force which is practised by large firms, but also partially by medium and small firms. To retain this system under conditions of major declines in the demand for labour, the Japanese government in 1975 introduced into the Employment Insurance Law an employment subsidy scheme under which one-half (in large enterprises) or two-thirds (in medium-sized and small enterprises) of the wage bill for excess labour was paid. During the period from January 1975 to October 1976, some 3.4 million workers received benefits under this programme, and the payroll subsidy covered 29 million man days. The subsidy proved to be very effective in keeping down the level of unemployment during the recession period. This subsidy scheme was revised in October 1977 and incorporated in the Employment Adjustment Services, a major component of the Employment Stabilisation Service. The subsidies are drawn from a special Employment Stabilisation Fund, which in contrast to the employment insurance programme is financed by the employers' contribution alone.

While the original subsidy programme was laid out primarily as an anti-depression scheme, the more recent emphasis has been rather on assisting structural change, e.g. the conversion of business activities, during which the employers are encouraged to maintain employment contracts with their employees. The subsidies are also granted to cover the costs of providing education and training while the employees remain with the enterprise or are shifted to other enterprises. These policies are in line with the general Japanese strategy of improving the viability of the private sector and not resorting to measures to absorb the unemployed into the public sector.

2. An overview of various national practices of job maintenance schemes is given in: F. Buttler, K. Gerlach, W. Sengenberger (ed.), Job Creation and Job Maintenance - Experience from Western Countries in the 1970s. Working Paper 1980-1, Arbeitskreis Sozialwissenschaftliche Arbeitsmarktforschung (SAMF), Paderborn, September 1980.

Another illustration of direct wage cost subsidy schemes to defer redundancies was the Temporary Employment Subsidy (TES) applied in the United Kingdom. TES is a 20 per cent wage subsidy to the employer of up to £20 per week, for as long as eighteen months, for each worker who would otherwise have been made redundant. It has had a disproportionately large impact on labour-intensive industries, such as textiles, clothing and footwear.(3) In these industries the scheme is being modified to deal with objections raised by other manufacturers in the European Economic Community according to which TES constituted an unfair subsidy programme in these industries, in violation of the General Agreement on Tariffs and Trade. Workers in these industries are now eligible under a short-time programme similar to the one practised in Germany (see below).

As in Japan, the British TES subsidy has been regarded as a temporary and transitional device to help the enterprise to revitalise its operation and market prospects rather than to maintain a firm with no future.

2. Temporary subsidies to short-time work - In Germany the public subsidy for partial compensation of lost earnings during short-time working has been of great importance since the incorporation of this allowance into the Labour Promotion Act of 1969.(4) During the recession of 1974 and 1975 short-time work was widespread in the economy to stabilise the level of employment and to avoid or defer redundancies. In 1974, the number of short-time workers was 292,000; in 1975, a peak volume of 773,000 workers was reached and the estimated reduction of unemployment through this measure was 175,000.

The rate of worker compensation during the short-time period is 68 per cent of the net wages lost and is thus equal to the unemployment benefit rate. To receive this compensation the employer (or the works council) must file an application with the local employment exchange office. It has to be demonstrated that the short-time work is "unavoidable", due to economic causes and temporary, and that all other available measures to forestall short-time work (like the elimination of overtime) have been taken. The scheme has been applied to cases of cyclical downturns, as well as to excess manpower resulting from rationalisation and restructuring measures.

Short-time subsidies are granted for a period of between four weeks and eighteen months (in areas of

---

3. Department of Employment Gazette, March 1978, Table 103; and July 1977, p. 694.
4. Bundesanstalt für Arbeit (J. Kühl, A.G. Paul, D. Blunk): Überlegungen II zu einer vorausschauenden Arbeitsmarktpolitik. Nürnberg, 1978.

structural depression or high unemployment for up to twenty four months) for a minimum of one-third of the work force losing 10 per cent or more of normal working time.

There are benefits from short-time work both to employers and the workers. The employer keeps his experienced work force and avoids the cost of dismissal and rehiring of workers. The workers retain their employment contract and benefit through reduced loss of earnings during short-time work. They receive their normal wage for the hours worked plus public short-time allowance for hours not worked, the sum of which varies between 68 and 99 per cent of normal earnings depending on the loss of hours per month and on the saving of taxes and other contributions. On average the compensation is somewhat more than 90 per cent of normal net pay.(5)

In France and Italy similar programmes of subsidised short-time work were introduced as a means of spreading employment. In France it is based on an agreement reached in 1975 between the National Council of Employers and trade union federations. For each hour lost below forty a week, a worker receives compensation for short-time work. When added to the state unemployment allowance, the allowance guarantees the worker at least 50 per cent of his normal gross hourly pay.

3. Subsidies to output, inventories or good purchase - Public programmes aimed at temporary maintenance of employment through short-term subsidies to promote production output, inventories or the purchase of goods during slack demand have been pioneered and are most advanced in Sweden. They constitute elements in an active labour market policy which together with anti-inflationary aggregate demand management and a solidaristic union wage policy compose what has become known as the "Rehn-Meidner Model" or the "Swedish Model".

In the main there are three types of measures applied in Sweden:

   a) Subsidies to government authorities and to local
      governments for purchases from Swedish manu-
      facturers

The purchase respite orders are subsidised by 20 per cent of the cost and have to be made earlier than originally planned, the idea being to gain time for the labour market authorities to find alternative solutions for the personnel affected. The firms supplying the products

5. H.R. Flechsenhar, "Kurzarbeit - Kosten und Finanzierung", Mitteilungen aus der Arbeitsmarkt- und Berufsforschung, No. 4, Nuremberg, 1978, p. 443.

must be located in areas suffering from unemployment or
the risk of unemployment.

A similar measure was followed in the shipbuilding
area. Swedish shipowners, when ordering ships from
Swedish shipyards, received a 30 per cent write-off loan
with no interest and no repayments for the first five
years. The remaining 70 per cent of the loan was financed
from government credits.

b) Subsidies to firms which build up their inventories during recession periods

In Sweden this measure was introduced under specific
circumstances and is no longer in operation. To be eligible for this subsidy of 20 per cent of the value of
inventory accumulation, a firm had to guarantee that the
number of workers in the firm did not decline during the
subsidisation period (of one year). Moreover, the firm
had to be situated in districts afflicted by heavy unemployment.

During the recession of 1976 to 1977 this subsidy
turned out to be the most expensive policy instrument,
with total costs exceeding 1,000 million Swedish crowns.
Among the prime beneficiaries of this subsidy were the
shipyards whose existence was threatneed mainly due to
the severe competition from shipbuilding in Japan.
Together with the public credit guarantees, the shipbuilding industries received public support running to a
total of 16.5 billion crowns from 1977 to 1981. Subsidies to inventories were also heavy in the steel and the
pulp and paper industries. In the pulp industry alone
the stocks had accumulated to 1.4 million tons of raw
materials, which made up half of the world's total storage
of this product.

The policy of building inventories helped for a
while. If the slump in the economy had proved to be
temporary, the policy would have been successful since
increased demand would have led to a buying up of the
stockpiles. As it turned out, unfortunately, the crisis
has been of a more permanent nature and new and more
drastic steps to deal with over-capacity had to be taken.

c) Subsidies for training of workers threatened
   by layoffs

If a Swedish firm withdraws plans for lay-offs and if
it designs a training programme, it can obtain subsidies
for up to 960 hours for each worker threatened by lay-
off. The training has to be vocation-oriented but can
include general training up to a maximum of 160 hours.
The subsidy amounts to 20 Swedish crowns per hour of
training.

<u>Problems of employment maintenance policies</u> - A number
of criticisms have been launched against the various public measures temporarily to maintain workers on the payroll. One major argument has been that the subsidies have
(to a considerable extent) amounted to windfall profits to
firms which would have kept the surplus workers on their
payroll in any case or would have built up their inventories even in the absence of subsidies. Another alleged
problem is a redistributional one. Subsidies may favour
the less efficient firms and may, therefore, distort
efficient resource allocation and competition. (This
misallocation would have to be compared to the one presented by low-capacity utilisation and by mass unemployment). Whatever the merits of these objections and criticisms, they would have to be balanced against the positive
impact of these measures as outlined above.(6)

Some of the problems may be traced to lack of administrative experience in implementing the schemes, given
the novelty of the measures. Another distinction that
helps sort out when employment-sustaining policies may be
appropriate is to define whether the economic changes
taking place are cyclical or secular. For cyclical changes
that is, short-run changes in the level of economic activity, some form of employment-sustaining policy makes
sense to tide the firm or industry over until the time
when demand rebounds for the products. However, if the
changes are basic and structural, what economists call a
secular development, then short-run measures only postpone
the inevitable. It is because of this realisation that
basic changes are taking place in so many industries and
so many countries that the judgement about employment
maintenance subsidies has frequently been negative.

APPROACHES IN SELECTED COUNTRIES

At this point we would like to compare the strategies
between several countries. Fortunately, we are able to
use the experience of one large multinational firm that
closed down facilities in five different countries during
the late 1970s. The various responses tend to reflect
differentiated national conditions.

<u>United States</u> - Many facilities have been closed by
this company. There has been some severance pay of a
modest amount, and for some workers advance notice of six

---

6. G. Schmid, "Wage-Cost Subsidy Programme in Germany
1974-75. Some circumstantial evidence of its impact and
effect - a quantitative study", Discussion papers 77-111,
International Institute of Management, Berlin 1977.

months has been given. In general, the workers have had a
mixed experience, with some finding employment when the
labour market was favourable and others remaining unemployed for a substantial period of time. This would be
laissez-faire with only modest concern for the transition
effects of the workers involved.

Great Britain - A large manufacturing facility was
closed down. The workers received redundancy pay averaging approximately £6,000. There were substantial demonstrations seeking to reverse the decision but this did not
happen. The workers were able to obtain other employment
in the greater-London labour market. This would be classified as laissez-faire with some concern for the financial
needs of the worker.

Sweden - When the company announced that it was
shutting down its facility in Sweden, the government
helped finance the loans that were required. This would
be a modified protection approach wherein the government
used its good offices and some capital but did not
nationalise or directly intervene to protect the jobs.

Tunisia - When the company announced to the government that it intended to close down its facility, the
government quickly passed legislation to buy the company
and to continue it in operation. This was in the face of
a weak position for domestic sales, since imports of this
product were capturing a larger and larger share of the
market. This approach would be considered pure protection
of the industry to avoid job loss.

Germany - In this case the facility was a warehouse
and sales operation and the close-down followed the normal
procedure of a close-down agreement, what is called a
social plan. The facility was closed and the union and
the workers involved agreed to a plan of payment and
assistance in obtaining other employment in the labour
market. This case would illustrate many of the elements
of what can be called the integrative approach.

THE INTEGRATIVE APPROACH

At this point we would like to summarise some of the
overriding themes that have emerged from our discussion
thus far. On the one hand, there is the strategy of
prevention: protecting jobs and employment stabilisation,
and this has been practised by a number of countries. It
emphasizes the premise that change per se may not be a
net benefit. Using balance sheets, the argument is made
that, if a particular industry is allowed to close down,
the economy may be worse off than if the particular industry were supported. By contrast, the strategy of

facilitating capital mobility works from the premise that the gains more than compensate for the losses; the losers may not be fully compensated but society in general will be better off via economic progress.

In between these two strategies is one that seeks to emphasize both the gains realised - from capital mobility as well as those from protecting the workers. Policies can be geared towards an active pursuit of programmes to enhance productivity and improve competitiveness by scrapping uncompetitive industries and firms and by promoting competitive and dynamic sectors. Underlying this approach is the belief that while structural change is inevitable and desirable, a pure market solution to change tends to produce social injury too high to be acceptable, or lead to a solution which places the cost or burden of the adjustment unilaterally on a particular group or party thus creating socially unfair solutions. To provide for a more even and more socially balanced distribution of the costs (and benefits) of structural adjustment, some intervention into the market process or some more co-operative procedure is required which helps to cushion the risks posed by employment dislocation for workers and communities. We call this latter approach the <u>integrative adjustment</u> method.

<u>Examples of the integrative approach</u> - Japan and Germany constitute two interesting cases of policies that we would call integrative. The strategic approaches in the two countries parallel each other more or less as far as the substantive thrust and objective of the approach is concerned. Both are directed towards modernising and rationalising the national economies, notably the industrial sectors, so as to strengthen their competitive power in world markets. Both countries lack energy and raw materials, and in the face of rapidly rising costs for these imports, Japan and Germany have been forced especially to compensate for the deteriorating terms of trade by maintaining or extending the export component of national production.

While the general objectives of restructuring policies between Japan and Germany are very similar, there are some striking differences as far as the institutional and organisational mechanisms are concerned. Thus, in Japan we find much more active and direct involvement of the government in orchestrating the process of industrial development. Industrial policy in Germany, in contrast, relies more on a decentralised, free-enterprise-type approach, leaving the basic responsibility of structural adaptation to the individual firm. The government intervenes in the process of structural change only to promote research and development and to cushion the risk of substantial damage in the shrinking sector. In the absence of direct and explicit state interventionism in Germany there is a comprehensive promotion of the general policy of modernisation based upon a fundamental consensus of the major social groups and some indirect public policies of economic restructuring.

Japan - Among the OECD countries, Japan today practises the most aggressive, forward-planning, approach to structural change. Rather than extending the life of uncompetitive or declining industries, the national government, in close co-operation with national banks and large corporations, fosters the rapid elimination of excess capacity and redirects financial and redundant labour resources into dynamic sectors. This practice is part of a comprehensive and well-established national economic planning policy, which deliberately gears resource allocation towards technological advance, energy saving, environmental protection and, above all, international competitiveness.

Recently, Japan's industry has entered a third major wave of investment since World War II. After developing the heavy industries and building up export-oriented mass production, investment into high technology and quality products is being promoted with public outlays of 240 billion yen under a seven-year national plan by the Ministry of Commerce and Industry (MITI).(7)

Among the growth industries are engineering, precision instruments and tools, electronics and information, motor vehicles, aircraft and aerospace industries. The major stagnating and shrinking branches are iron and steel, textiles, non-ferrous metals and shipbuilding.

Financial assistance and promotion, ranging from development credits, to subsidies, tax credits and financial aid for and co-ordination of research and development, are provided primarily to the industrial sector, which is considered to be of major strategic significance for the international competitiveness of Japanese industry. In 1978, legislation was passed that explicitly promotes the introduction and spread of high technology.

At the same time as the dynamic sector receives the attention and support of national planning, so do the shrinking industries or those which are the least competitive. By a 1978 law the state provides for "extraordinary measures to stabilise declining industries". The objective is to force these industries to shrink in order to improve their chances of survival. The procedures laid down encompass rules on how to identify candidates for capacity reduction, methods to determine the rate of decline and rules and methods of how to finance

7. "The Visions of MITI Policies in the 1980s", in News from MITI, 17 March 1980.

the contraction process (at present shipbuilding, steel, some chemical products and textiles are designated as contraction industries).

The decision about where and how to cut down on production capacity is influenced by consulting teams composed of representatives of industry and the ministries. The financing of the cost of capacity reduction and for the severance payments to displaced workers is based on loans provided largely by the state-owned Japanese Development Bank.(8)

To dampen the rise of protectionism against Japanese imports into Western countries, the Japanese have started a policy of joint ventures in their major export target countries. Under this policy the Japanese companies seek to limit their export activities to supplying investment goods and component parts, and leaving major production to plants in the host foreign countries.

Germany - In Germany, as mentioned, the thrust of industrial policy has also been to modernise and rationalise industry so as to maintain and extend international competitiveness. In contrast to Japan, however, the state intervenes less in the process of change in the industrial structure. Instead, the course of structural change is much more left to market forces.

The state, in principle, limits its engagement in the adjustment process to the general promotion of capital and labour and to issuing rules and standards which have to be observed by private industry. Exceptions to this rule are made where the market process generates abrupt development, large frictions or other socially unacceptable outcomes, as has been the case for the steel and shipbuilding industries. In shipbuilding, a conversion of the product programme in the direction of diversification and specialisation has been facilitated by state subsidies and loans. Similarly, in the steel industry modernisation and reorganisation have been promoted in areas which face disadvantages in terms of their location relative to suppliers and markets.

With respect to some of the troubled industries, national industrial policies are superseded more and more by international policy-making. Thus, there have been growing efforts during recent years to develop common industrial policies throughout the EEC. Such policies tend to have a strongly interventionist slant, including the determination of production or capacity-quotas, subsidies for maintaining operations in some regions of the EEC, and minimum or recommended prices for products. At present, such EEC plans are in force in the basic steel

---

8. OECD Economic Surveys: Japan, July 1980, pp. 48 ff.

and synthetic fibres industries which specify a planned reduction of capacity as well as production and sales quotas.

In the area of social policies the Commission of the EEC has proposed such measures as the reduction of weekly working hours, expansion of part-time work, introduction of a fifth shift, early retirement and limits to overtime work.

Special incentives are provided as part of German industrial policies for industries which are regarded as being of key importance for future technological advancement, and for enterprises undertaking investments of general interest but with a high risk for returns, as is the case for the aerospace industry. Such incentives are based either on tax reduction for research and development or on direct grants for particular projects. Most of these incentives are of limited duration and have a declining scale of payments.

To facilitate the growth of the export-oriented, high technological sector of the German economy (including machine tools, equipment, vehicles, chemicals and electronics) the state has also promoted training of the labour force with the objective of improving average skill levels. Despite increased unemployment, aggregate shortages have continued to exist for skilled workers in the face of more sophisticated technology and the need for rapid reorientation towards new developments in the product market. Skilled workers, it is felt, exhibit greater abilities to accommodate to these new conditions.

While in comparison to Japan the state in Germany keeps a much lower profile in directing the course of industrial development, there has been a similar widespread consensus among business, trade unions and the government that the modernisation strategy is of vital significance for maintaining economic growth and social security. This social consensus has supported co-operation between the major groups on the enterprise level as well as on the industry and macro levels of economic and industrial policy. One might conceive of this co-operation as a kind of productivity deal in which both labour and capital earn benefits from productivity improvement. The workers receive high wages and social security in return for their readiness to go along with a productivity policy. Correspondingly, the employers' quid pro quo is the co-operation of labour in industrial change, in return for the employers' making of commitments to worker participation and worker security.

V

APPROACHES TO INTEGRATIVE ADJUSTMENT

In this chapter we complete the shift in emphasis to the employment side of the equation. We will not ignore completely the capital side but it will be only considered in relation to the employment side of the picture.

Having established the notion of an integrative strategy, one that reconciles both capital and labour considerations, we can consider four programme areas for carrying out the integrative approach. The four categories can be classified in terms of the earlier distinction between internal and external changes and between emphasis on jobs and on workers.

The following figure lays out the four possibilities:

		Target of Programmes	
		Jobs	Workers
Forms of restructuring	Internal	Enterprise viability	Human resource techniques
	External	Regional development	Labour market re-engagement

Since we will devote a separate section of the report to each of these programme areas, we will confine ourselves at this point to some introductory comments.

Internal restructuring can focus on either jobs or workers (or a combination of the two). The focus on jobs, what we call enterprise viability, may involve an improved organisation and utilisation of productive resources and, as a result of cost saving, gaining or regaining profitability and competitiveness or the adjustment of capacity to business fluctuation. A fair proportion of the productivity bargains concluded in Britain during the period of incomes policy in the 1960s and 1970s fit into this category.(1) Another case in point is represented by the reorganisation of the Swedish shipbuilding industry in the 1970s in reaction to increased competition from Japan. In Sweden the objective was to increase productivity both through mergers of shipbuilding operations and through taking an assembly-line approach to production.

By contrast, the focus on workers means the continued utilisation of the existing work force as a result of using a variety of human resources planning and programme techniques. Japan stands out among the industrialised nations in practising this type of internal conversion approach very effectively within its large industrial enterprises. The emphasis given to internal adjustment is related to the practice of life-term employment, especially in large enterprises. Despite a career employment relationship for a large proportion of their employees, Japanese firms manage to achieve considerable flexibility in the deployment of the work force through internal worker mobility, change of worker assignment, and expensive reliance upon company education and training. The human resource approach in Japan is promoted by institutional/industrial relations factors which foster bargaining and conflict resolution on the enterprise level. One such factor is the enterprise-based labour union.

The external approach to jobs emphasizes the creation of new employment in the same regions where some industries are declining so that employment is available to ameliorate with what would otherwise be a situation of high structural unemployment. Regional policy involves promoting the growth of highly productive and competitive industries.

With respect to the adjustment of labour on the workers side, the corresponding policies are usually termed labour market or manpower policies. They aim at cushioning the loss of jobs for workers, firms and communities, and facilitating the transition to new employment by income maintenance, training and retraining.

A. ENHANCING THE VIABILITY OF THE ENTERPRISE

The first of the four programmes that we would like to consider in some detail comes from that corner of the

---

1. Robert B. McKersie and L.C. Hunter, Pay, Productivity and Collective Bargaining, Macmillan, London, 1973.

matrix where the emphasis is on internal restructuring, that is, workers stay with the same company or enterprise, and large-scale work force displacements are either prevented or minimised by enhancing the viability of the enterprise. Something is done to make the operations of the business more competitive.

The variations on this theme are many and can be categorised as follows. First, there are the changes to the cost structure of operations as they exist. We limit our consideration to those measures that stem from employee/union initiatives or have some relationship to the worker side of the organisation. One response that appears to be occurring more and more frequently in the United States as economic restructuring threatens more and more jobs is that of "rollbacks" in established wages and fringe benefits. A second category, and one that also operates on the cost side of the existing enterprise, involves productivity improvement - we are especially interested in those that emerge through labour-management discussions. Both rollbacks and productivity improvements have the potential for lowering costs to the point that the jobs which might have been in jeopardy can be saved, at least for the short run, or perhaps even for a longer period of time.

Another programme that protects jobs for incumbent workers can be labelled alternate products for the operation that is in jeopardy. Some companies approach the challenge of restructuring from the viewpoint that their existing work force and their attachment to the local community are assets to be tapped and related to new business ventures. This approach will be illustrated for both the United Kingdom and the United States; and the approach also appears to be emerging in several other countries.

The final possibility we term "re-planting" of operations. In situations where economic change represents an updating of plant and equipment, the location decision about the modernised facility can consider the existing labour market area as a leading alternative.

Throughout this section we will be attentive to certain patterns or differences that exist across countries with respect to enhancing the viability of the enterprise. In some cases the action will be taken early on, while in other cases the remedial steps will only be taken later as the crisis deepens. Also, we can distinguish between efforts that are aimed at protecting a core of remaining jobs, and efforts to protect employment for all workers. Generally speaking, efforts in the United Kingdom and France appear to fall into the second category whereas there are many examples in Germany, the United States and Japan that fall into the first category.

For example, the development of the Jamestown, New York Labor-Management Committee came only after a long period of job loss and the emerging conviction on the part of key leaders in the community that the challenge facing them was to enhance the viability of the remaining businesses rather than just try to find new businesses to fill the vacant factories that had occupied the scene for some time. Similarly, a very active productivity improvement programme is currently under way at Crucible Steel in the United States, aimed at keeping Crucible solvent and protecting the jobs that remain - a substantial reduction from those that this company numbered in the early 1970s before the shakeout occurred in the steel industry.

Rollback of Established Wages and/or Benefits

This response to impending displacements appears to have occurred mainly in the United States and primarily during the past several years. While no precise statistics are available, it is estimated that at least 50 instances of rollbacks have occurred in order to prevent job loss. By far the most publicised and the most important has been the series of cuts that Chrysler workers have accepted, as part of the refinancing and survival programme for this major auto company. Estimates for the latest rounds of cuts puts the annual cost per worker at somewhere between $3,000 and $6,000 per year. These cuts represent reductions in existing take-home pay, as well as a freeze of projected increases in cost-of-living adjustments.

Most of the rollbacks that have been implemented have occurred in industries such as steel and rubber which have faced severe economic problems. The form of the rollbacks is usually a freeze on anticipated benefits at a future date. For example, at Uniroyal, workers took a cut of $0.58 an hour for the last five months in 1980 and deferred an upcoming cost-of-living increase, with the parties agreeing that "give backs" would be restored at future dates during the life of the agreement.

Generally speaking, workers and their local union leaders are more willing to consider rollbacks than top union leadership. This is because the impact of the trade-offs differs as between the local and central levels. Members are more concerned about jobs and, when it appears that a plant shutdown is in the offing, they are much more willing to offer up concessions. By contrast, central union leadership, concerned about the stability of the pattern and being afraid that one breakthrough will force them to accede to others, tend to be much more resistant to these deviations. For example, the workers at Kaiser Steel voted recently to accept a range of concessions; yet this package was disapproved by the United

Steelworkers leadership in Pittsburgh. Another illustration would be the staunch opposition by the top Union of Auto Workers (UAW) leadership to reopening contracts with General Motors and Ford – they have tried to isolate what they have done at Chrysler as a response to a very special situation and they are resisting any move by these other companies to negotiate similar concessions.

The willingness of unions to go along with rollbacks is related to the probability of demise. The closer to the "brink", the more ready are the workers and top union leaders to accept some job-saving concessions. Thus, Braniff Airlines, experiencing substantial financial difficulties, has had no difficulty in getting its workers to accept a pay cut. The workers at the Bridge Division of United States Steel, having voted in the negative about concessions, changed their minds when the company announce that it was going ahead with plans to shut the plant down.

Productivity Bargaining

This approach to avoiding job loss has been practised quite heavily in the United Kingdom (2) over the past two decades and has been increasingly important in the United States. As mentioned earlier, we can find examples in other countries such as Sweden.

To capture the flavour of this approach, as it is presently practised, it is helpful to consider a few examples. In the United States the United Rubber workers have agreed in a number of cases to abandon piece work, to accept continuous shift operations and to conduct operations at weekends without special premium pay. All of these steps enable the new capital equipment, especially for radial tyre production, to be much more fully utilised. Turning to the United Kingdom, at the Glengarnock works of British Steel the skilled work force recently agreed to drop all demarcation barriers among the different crafts as a way of preventing the closing of the plant, thereby saving several hundred jobs.

The function of productivity bargaining, as can be seen from the foregoing examples, is to achieve a better match between the work organisation, the deployment of the work force and the technological requirements of the operations. In some cases the adjustment is fairly minor; in other cases it is quite major and represents a type of surgery – cutting away a whole series of practices that have grown up over time and impede the full utilisation of plant and equipment.

---

2. R.B. McKersie and L. Hunter, Pay, Productivity and Collective Bargaining, Macmillan, London, 1973.

The results from productivity bargaining have
generally been positive: productivity has improved.
Whether the improvement is enough to save the jobs over
the long run is another question. In many instances the
net effect of productivity bargaining is to give the operation a lease of life, but the overriding competitive and
environmental circumstances may be too adverse for the
enterprise to survive indefinitely.

The important question to be asked is the following:
What is the range for improving the viability of the operation through productivity bargaining and how does this
potential contribution compare to the overall gap that
exists between the plant in question and competition elsewhere? In a number of instances, workers and unions have
been motivated to improve operations through productivity
bargaining and have made a substantial contribution - only
to learn that the problem was much bigger than the improvements they worked so hard to achieve. This leads to
considerable worker frustration. For example, in the
case of several plants of British Steel slated to be
closed, local groups have worked hard to improve operations, thinking that such efforts would make a difference, only to learn that the inland location rendered
these operations obsolete. The same sequence of hope,
problem solving, shutdown and bitterness has been played
out at the Youngstown Works of United States Steel, where
a local programme under the direction of the plant
manager, with the full co-operation of the workers and
local union, succeeded in lowering costs substantially
but, again, was not enough to keep the operation from
being closed down.

In summary, productivity bargaining can be seen as
a useful tool where the competitive problems are not
procedurally immense. We will have more to say about the
important process aspects of productivity bargaining later
on when we talk about the participation of workers and
their representatives in maintaining the viability of the
enterprise.

Development of Alternative Plans

An approach that has been tried quite regularly in
Japan (e.g. shipbuilding) is the development of alternate
products or new enterprises to which excess workers can
be transferred. In the case of Japan this is made
feasible by the conglomerate nature of many of the large
corporations.

The idea has been pushed with some passion in
Britain. For example, a group of shop stewards at Lucas
Aircraft spent several years compiling a compendium of
ideas that the company could engage in as a way of preventing massive dismissal. But no new products were

introduced and Lucas has continued to shed labour. It is
instructive to review the employment decline of Lucas
Aerospace. In 1970 it employed 18,000 workers. By 1974
employment was down to 13,000. It was during this period
when the combine was developed and presented an alternate
corporate plan to the company which was rejected. In 1977
a labour surplus of 1,000 jobs was announced. Total employment in 1978 was down to 12,000 and at that time the company announced additional redundancies. These cutbacks
were curtailed after considerable protest, but in June 1980
the company proceeded to implement 2,000 redundancies.
By 1981 employment was under 10,000, almost half of what
it had been ten years earlier.

    In the United States, several examples can be cited
of companies having taken the initiative to find products
that have had the net effect of keeping existing work
forces occupied. For example, International Silver, when
it went out of the business of producing tableware, looked
around the Connecticut area and decided that it could
enter the stainless tubing and assembly-equipment re-
fitting businesses. It retrained several hundred craftsmen and, as a result, has been able to continue manufacturing operations in a community where it represents
a "household name". Similarly, the Winnebago Company,
maker of recreational vehicles, has mailed out a 35-page
booklet describing its manufacturing capabilities to 1,000
large companies in the United States and has received a
variety of sub-contract orders, thereby keeping a good
number of its workers employed.

    But the above examples are the exceptions rather than
the rule. In most instances, management is not interested,
nor does it feel that it is competent to enter into new
lines of business solely for the purpose of keeping its
existing work force occupied. Where this approach is, in
fact, pursued, there seem to be a number of facilitating
factors. For one, management feels a commitment to provide
continuity of employment for the current work force and to
remain in the local community. Second, management possesse
an entrepreneurial spirit which means that it is willing to
go out and look for new business and take the high risk of
getting into new lines of work. Finally, some type of
capital infusion must be available from retained earnings
or from financial institutions.

    Thus, it would seem that where employment continuity
is considered a must, as it is for many regular workers
in Japan, companies will reach for this alternative as a
way of making good on their mandate. However, in
countries such as the United States where such a commitment is not manifest, the use of this alternative will be
quite rare.

    A good summary of the perfunctory way in which this
alternative is considered can be seen in the following

announcement when a large company closed a Scottish plant in mid-1977. "We have investigated the possibility of putting new products into the plant and a considerable amount of detailed work has been done, but projections finally showed that there would not be sufficient business in the foreseeable future. There is therefore no alternative but to close the factory in mid-1977".(3)

Replanting of Facilities in Existing Areas

This programme option addresses the question: Should the new facility be located in a new or in the existing geographical area? The assumption is that restructuring often means that the plant will be modernised and altered to the extent that it essentially represents a new operation. Certainly, in some industries such as steel, where there is an integrated complex, modernisation may only apply to a part of the facility, e.g. the coke ovens or the blast furnace - consequently, the new operations have to be physically located on the same premises.

Our interest is in those situations where the potential of some digression exists. A good example of this would be the automobile industry, where a new parts plant or an assembly operation could be located almost anywhere. In fact, given the modern layout of an auto plant, which requires a lot of space on one floor, it is probably preferable for the plant to be located in a "green field" site and away from existing facilities (which are usually in crowded urban areas). Quite significantly, a number of instances have occurred where new facilities have been constructed near old facilities, when the company might have preferred to locate the operation on a "green field" site. For example, General Motors, in closing down its Cadillac assembly plant in Detroit, committed itself to remain in the Detroit area and currently is in the process of obtaining a parcel of 300 acres through urban renewal arrangements in the centre of Detroit. General Tyre has committed itself to the union and the community to build its next new tyre facility in Akron, Ohio. Similarly, Goodyear has said that it will build a small rubber plant to meet the needs of its laboratory facility in Akron.

In other cases, the building of new plants commenced without employment commitments, but through collective bargaining the parties developed transition arrangements. For example, Ford Motor closed down an iron foundry as part of its River Rouge complex. The workers were given transfer rights to a new casting plant at Flat Rock, approximately 25 miles away. Similarly, in the Cincinnati area, transfer arrangements have been developed between a terminated transmission plant and some new facilities being established in the same geographical area.

---

3. Taken from an unpublished study by John Purcell, Manchester Business School, 1977.

The replanting of the new facilities in the same area represents a clear gain for the current work force. It also represents a gain for the community and in some ways this latter dimension is the dominant factor. The decision of General Motors to remain in Detroit must be seen in terms of its headquarters location in that city and its close identification with Detroit as the automobile capital of the world. As far as union leaders are concerned, if they know that the new plant will be organised (and this is certainly the case with the automobile industry in the United States), they are probably indifferent as to whether the new plant is in the old area or in some new area of the country.

The choice is less readily available in Europe or Japan, where space for new facilities is not readily available, where there is much more pressure to provide continuity of employment for existing workers, and where changes - modernisation arrangements - take place more slowly and are more likely to be done to existing operations rather than the development of new facilities from scratch.

B. THE MANAGEMENT OF HUMAN RESOURCES

This section considers another internal technique. This time, instead of the emphasis being on the job or cost side of the enterprise, the attention shifts directly to the work force and methods employed to assure continuity of employment, while at the same time achieving the advantages of change and restructuring. This approach has received various labels such as continuity of employment, full employment and deployment of available human resources.

In essence, the approach protects the individual by maintaining the worker's employment, even though the job or operation has been eliminated or rearranged. In most of Europe this approach is followed assiduously; and a combination of legislation, collective bargaining agreements and social understandings discourage or even prohibit firms from laying off or declaring workers redundant. For example, in the European Coal and Steel Community enterprises are required to make efforts to insure that "no interruption in employment occurs".

Even in the United States, where there has been much less willingness to avoid lay-off and where, in the face of cyclical (and certainly in the face of secular) changes, companies quickly export the instability to the larger labour market, there appears to be a growing interest in the use of human resource techniques for avoiding as much as possible these disruptions in the continuity of employment. For example, a number of large companies, such as IBM and others in the high technology industries, have stated as a matter of basic personnel policy that they will do everything possible to maintain continuity of employment. In essence, these companies view job security as a number-one business objective.

Then, too, it must be noted that in many situations the principle of attrition has been followed de facto, because the size of the work force in many companies and industries has been steadily reduced over an extended period of time. Typically, the number of workers affected by the final shutdown represents only a small fraction of these employed at the peak. We do not have complete data to buttress our contention about the slow deterioration process; but our surmise is that during the 10- or 15-year period preceding the actual plant shutdown, a combination of attrition and staged lay-offs occurred, so that the final complement is only a small portion of the total number of people who have been affected by the deterioration process. In this sense, some form of human resource management has been practised as these enterprises have come slowly down the "slopes of decline".

A number of studies have demonstrated that for most European countries employment levels are much more stable than would otherwise be indicated, given the ups and downs of the economy. Specifically, for Japan, Germany and some other OECD countries there is comparatively little connection between the cyclical performance of the economy and changes in employment levels. However, it is one thing for employment to be stabilised in the face of cyclical changes; it is another for this to happen in the face of very basic secular changes. And this is the challenge that human resource management attempts to meet. In the face of vast and pervasive restructuring, enterprises are able to avoid lay-off by a variety of human resource policies and programmes.

Background Factors

There are several reasons why an emphasis on human resource management has become important in dealing with the consequences of economic restructuring. Certainly, from a historical point of view the movement towards career employment has been steady and uninterrupted. Only 20 or 30 years ago in the United States, for example, considerable emphasis was placed on paying people by the hour or even by shorter unit measures, namely, piece-work reimbursement. Then, as companies became larger and orientation changed, a shift took place away from piece-work and towards salary systems and even in some cases, as a result of the interest of unions, in the direction of guaranteed annual employment programmes. But, regardless of the label placed on the development, the movement has been towards the view that workers are employed by the enterprise for an extended period of time. This development has been carried to its ultimate for about half of the workers in the Japanese economy, who enjoy career employment with their parent company.

Economists prefer to explain this development in terms of quasi-fixed human capital and the advantages accruing to both sides from an orientation to career employment. In Europe the development has also been spurred by legislation and various other incentives that have shaped the employment relationship. For example, inducements have come from protection instituted against dismissal and downgrading and from public policies of job maintenance. To the extent that these efforts have imposed legal restriction on work force reduction (lay-offs) or have increased the cost of lay-offs, they have contributed to the fixed-cost character of labour and, thus, have contributed to a more careful and long-term orientation of businesses towards human resource management.

For example, in a survey on the impact of employment protection legislation in the United Kingdom, some of the managers held that, as a result of these legal requirements, they devoted more attention to human resources and were more systematic and explicit in their evaluation and use of human resources. Job specification, selection and appraisal of performance had been improved and more regard was paid to ensuring that people were properly trained. Personnel considerations were more salient and the influence of the personnel function had increased.(4)

Evidence for this proposition concerning the upgrading of human resources management as a result of job security measures and worker participation in personnel planning is also available for Germany. It has been shown that firms with well-developed systems of personnel planning and worker co-determinati n had lower rates of work force reduction during the recession of 1974-1975. And, the firms practising personnel planning were less prone to resort to dismissals during economic downturns. Instead, they used softer measures, like recruitment freeze, severance pay contracts and early retirement to lower the size of their work force. In addition, greater emphasis was placed in these firms on varying working time (through overtime and short-time work) and on stabilising the work volume or creating new demand for manpower, through such measures as building up inventories,

---

4. W.W. Daniel and E. Store, The Impact of Employment Protection Laws, Policy Studies Institute, Vol. XLIV, No. 577, London, June 1978.

increased training, and preventive repair and maintenance work.(5)

Programme Techniques for Achieving Continuity of Employment

Conceptually, the various measures that are used by firms to implement a programme of human resource management can be divided into three categories. The first deals with the direct reduction of the number of workers needed. In some ways this can be viewed as the management of excess personnel. The second broad category has to do with balancing the amount of work available to the number of persons on hand. Finally, there are a series of measures that are aimed at moving personnel to other sections of the business or to other lines of work in order to keep them productively employed.

Reducing the number of workers - Firms in Germany and Japan quickly engage in what has been called hiring stops, not filling vacancies or reducing the number of new recruits. For large German firms about 60 per cent resort to this method. For Japanese firms it is even higher, over 70 per cent. Another technique that is used more and more frequently, especially in Germany, is that of early retirement. This has not been used as frequently in Japan where the retirement age is built into the career employment situation.

1. Use of a hiring stop - The advantages of this measure can be quickly summarised. They are the general advantages of any human resource management programme, namely, enhancing the morale and putting confidence in the current organisation to be able to handle the challenges that are ahead. The disadvantages involve the loss of "new blood" and the fact that shortages will develop in certain high turnover occupations - as a result some people will be required to work overtime and there will be a general feeling of fatigue when it is not possible to hire replacements to help with the workload.

2. Early retirement - Depending upon the demography of the work force, it may be possible to achieve a reduction in the number of personnel through the institution of early retirement. Some organisations are top heavy with long-service workers. For example, it has been estimated that the United States Post Office, which is facing some dramatic changes in technology and style of

---

5. R. Schultz-Wild, Betriebliche Beschäftigungs-politik in der Krise, Frankfurt/Main, New York, Campus, 1978; W. Sengenberger, Protection of Workers in Case of Work Force Reduction in the Undertaking - The Case of the Federal Republic of Germany, A Report to the ILO, Geneva, August 1979.

operations, has approximately 40 per cent of its work force in the over-50 age group, thereby giving it considerable potential for bringing about a rapid reduction in the number of personnel employed.

The Ford Motor Company of Germany recently induced about 10 per cent of its workers to retire on a voluntary early retirement programme. Early retirement schemes are widely spread in the German coalmining and steel industries where, under social plans, workers may retire at an age of 59 or less.

One of the big drawbacks to this approach is that often the best people are lost as a result of an early retirement programme. This is true of any voluntary programme: the company cannot control who steps forward to accept the proposal of early retirement. For example, in the case of the French steel companies, the 50,000 franc programme was subscribed to mainly by younger skilled workers. Finally, the concept of early retirement is becoming increasingly difficult to implement since it is not in line with societal trends that permit people to continue working longer and longer. As a result, in some countries, people who take early retirement move on to start another career.

Various measures to balance the operations - One can envisage the adjustments as a type of priority list. The first item is the reduction of overtime. For large German firms 100 per cent institute this measure, while for comparable Japanese firms about 80 per cent do so.

The next step, and one that is a natural buffer, is the recall of sub-contract work. For large German firms, over 50 per cent institute this measure. The IBM Corporation attempts to buffer its inside employment on a one-to-one basis for the work that is in the hands of sub-contractors. The Boeing Corporation, after its bad experience with cutbacks in the 1970s, increased the amount of sub-contracting from 30 to 50 per cent of all its activities.

A third line of defence has to do with work sharing. For large German firms over 70 per cent follow this procedure by introducing short-time work during periods of slack. In the United States, work sharing is not used as much, since most workers would prefer to have the junior members on lay-off, drawing some type of unemployment insurance, while the more senior workers continue to work full schedules.

It must be recognised that short-time working only serves as a temporary solution; and as is the case for most other devices mentioned in this chapter, in the context of large-scale work force displacements, work sharing represents a "holding action" until attrition and other ways of reducing the permanent size of the work force can be instituted.

Finally, the last line of defence involves moving work to where available workers are employed by the company. Few instances of this measure can be found, although IBM and several other full employment companies will institute this measure as a last resort.

Out-placement of personnel - Japanese firms appear to be the most frequent practitioners of transferring workers to subsidiaries, to other plants, or to elsewhere within the enterprise. About 60-70 per cent of the large enterprises use this measure. The practice is not as prevalent in Germany and does not exist too frequently in other OECD countries.

Generally speaking, workers do not like to change their place of employment. They are even less willing to change their place of residence. Consequently, unless the alternative is lay-off, very few workers are likely to volunteer for redeployment to other employment/ residential situations. For example, Lord Robens talks about how difficult it was to get mine workers to move from one pit to another, and many of them would rather have accepted redundancy payments. "Miners at closing pits would not go near our employment vans for fear of being offered suitable alternate employment, and thereby losing their redundancy payments".(6)

On the other hand, a number of recent experiences from Japan and Germany suggest that if management is on "top of the situation" it may be possible to transfer workers as a way of avoiding lay-off. For example, in the work and loan programme used in Japan, steelworkers who have been displaced have been reassigned to work in car factories. In the case of Germany the firm of Daimler-Benz also has used the "loan" concept. Specifically, a group of workers from a shipbuilding firm is working temporarily in the car concern.

Evaluation of Human Resource Management

Where human resource measures can be employed, they appear to work effectively and they can make a substantial difference in the number of people who are actually displaced. Clearly, certain circumstances facilitate the use of such techniques. Where the pace and nature of the change is such that the displacement is gradual, then a much more efficient application of the techniques can

---

6. Alfred Robens, Ten Year's Stint, Cassell, London, 1972, p. 105.

take place. The steady introduction of new technology, the shift to larger plants on a gradual basis - these represent circumstances wherein human resource management can make its mark. However, if the loss of markets takes place rapidly, if an out-moded plant needs to be abandoned, if there is no employment base left within which to bring about the reallocations, the scope for these measures is much more limited.

Another facilitating condition is financial support in the form described earlier under employment stabilisation policies. Given the need to "bide time" until attrition can absorb the excess workers, it may be necessary for the firm to receive financial support from government to hold people who would otherwise be displaced. Another key ingredient is the skill of management in laying out the data and techniques for achieving human resources objectives. For example, the following list describes the role of personnel planning in the German steel industry and this list could be applied more generally as a requirement for making this approach work.

Instruments of personnel planning in the German steel industry:(7)

1. Extensive data banks on personnel and jobs.
2. Short-term, medium-term and long-term projections on sales, production capacity, capacity utilisation, and need for labour.
3. Intra- and inter-company co-ordination of plans on vocational training, anti-cyclical policies on vocational training in line with federal and state policies.
4. Working committees for the exchange of information among companies on sales, employment, output, working time and earnings.
5. Joint labour-management committees on economic and personnel planning in accordance with Sections 12 and 106 of the Plant Constitution Act. Combination of information and consultation of employment measures.
6. Joint planning of working time, vacation, workers assignment, short-time work, overtime working, and transfer.

   - Extensive social plans in case of work force reductions.
   - Ergonomic committees in accordance with Sections 90 and 91 of the Plant Constitution Act; including consultation between management and labour over quality of work criteria and safety for new plants.

---

7. H. Hagenbruck, "Personalplanung in einem Unternehmen der Montanindustrie", in: M. Maase, R. Schultz-Wild (eds.) Personalplanung zwischen Wachstum und Stagnation, Campus, Frankfurt/New York, 1980.

Finally, a positive response from the unions involved helps make human resource planning techniques operate more effectively. But this stance is not always
present. In some countries, many union leaders prefer to
have the workers accept redundancy or for the union to
negotiate a special severance pay plan (wherein the union
leaders can demonstrate the benefits they have achieved on
behalf of the workers about to be displaced). A human
resource management programme does not present visible
gains that labour leaders can be associated with, and they
may feel very uncomfortable watching a work force and
their membership slowly shrink into oblivion. Nevertheless, the rank and file usually prefer a gradual decline
to redundancies and for this reason most union leaders
"look the other way", when management adopts the strategy
of reducing the work force by attrition.

Examples of Human Resource Management

We close this section with some illustrations of
human resource measures from the two countries where the
approach appears to be most fully developed: Germany and
Japan.

Germany - An interesting example of human resource
management occurred several years ago when Opel reduced
employment by 10 per cent in the face of a 20 per cent
cut in output. The 5,000 excess workers fell into two
categories: about half (2,300) took early retirement,
age 59 and above, and received one year's extra pay as
severance. Approximately 3,000 younger workers were
severed with a "golden handshake". In the case of Ford,
the cost per worker severed was almost $13,000. The
management of Roechling-Burbach, a division of Arbed,
negotiated a social plan with the union that provided for
the displacement of approximately 8,000 individuals.
Many in this group were covered by early retirement programmes which provided special severance pay and bridging
payments until normal retirement arrangements would take
effect.

Japan - Examples of redeployment by human resource
management are quite numerous. For example, over the
decade of the 1970s employment in coalmining dropped from
over 100,000 to 37,000 with 80 per cent of the displacements taking place into other businesses within the same
conglomerate groups.

In shipbuilding, where there have been substantial
declines of the magnitude of 60,000 workers, early retirement and hiring freeze programmes have been relied
on heavily. Many workers have been supported until they
could find other jobs. The number who have actually
been laid off has been a small fraction of the total number who have been transferred or allowed to leave via
normal attrition.

Another example comes from Nippon Steel. About ten years ago employment was over 85,000 and today it is down to 70,000. This reduction has taken place without lay-offs - with a number of people shifting to other industries. More importantly, about 1,000 workers have been loaned to the booming automobile industry.

C. LABOUR MARKET RE-ENGAGEMENT

With this section we come to policies and programmes that deal with external restructuring. Remembering the earlier discussion about the essence of external restructuring, this strategy occurs against a backdrop where economic changes require the shifting of workers from the declining to the growing industries. The changes are of such a pace and such a scope that workers cannot be accommodated within the existing industries, either through competitive improvements or through slow phase-out strategies.

Of the countries in the study, probably the United States makes most frequent use of this strategy. Today, the number of workers in the United States who face the need for re-engagement is much larger than those who have been laid off as a result of plant shutdowns. We are referring to several hundred thousand who have been laid off "subject to recall" but will never be recalled. Not all workers who are laid off end up being candidates for redeployment. Indeed, over several decades the tradition of lay-off "subject to recall" has developed wherein approximately two-thirds to three-quarters of workers laid-off in manufacturing can expect recall, usually within several months. However, this situation has changed and many workers on long-term lay-off from auto, steel and rubber find themselves, de facto, in the category of permanently displaced.

As with the previous section where the emphasis was on the worker and on programmes to help the worker (as distinguished from the emphasis on the job side) we will consider various measures that are undertaken to help workers re-engage with other employment. Various perspectives or roles in this process can be identified. First, there is government and its agencies, there is the employer of "last repose", and finally, there is the worker and his or her resourcefulness.

Overview of the Process of Re-engagement

Conceptually, the readjustment or re-engagement process can be divided into several steps. First, there is the important step of targeting jobs and developing

jobs to which the displacees can be moved. We will consider for the most part this subject subsequently, as part
of the next section dealing with regional economic
development policies and efforts by government agencies
and other groups to secure employment opportunities for
those leaving declining industries.

The second step deals with the motivation and prep-
aration of displaced workers to move into the labour market and to seek other employment. In this category, we
include a variety of counselling and "hands on" programmes
that instil motivation and equip the worker to make the
transition. Training programmes play an especially important role.

Next, we consider the linkages that make it possible
for workers to identify opportunities and, if necessary,
to move geographically to obtain new employment. This
step involves the "good offices" in the employment service
and other agencies that will help workers move from one
job to another.

The above steps all deal with the substantive process of re-engagement. There are two other important
procedural or threshold conditions. One of these is the
subject of notice and consultation that provides a period
of time for planning during which the workers can confront the reality of the change and their representatives
can negotiate social plans. One other key facilitating
condition is income support, often referred to as redundancy payment or severance programmes. Here we will be
considering various arrangements to cushion the economic
loss that is inherent during the transition period.

Hiring Displacees

Since the purpose of any readjustment programme is
to achieve re-employment of the displacees, we consider
those measures that target this group for special attention. In a later section we will consider programmes
aimed at job creation (with the presumption - not necessarily true in practice - that the new position will benefit the displacees).

Japan - In Japan a number of public measures were
legislated in 1978 to assist the re-employment of workers
displaced from the structurally depressed industries and
areas. The industries and areas were designated by the
Ministry of Labour in close consultation with ministries
responsible for industrial policy. As of August 1980,
the industries designated include textiles, sections of
iron and steel, aluminium refining and shipbuilding.

Under these new programmes, employers who have hired
as regular workers those displaced from the selected

depressed industries and who have conducted their education and training for them, receive payroll subsidies
of between one-half and two-thirds (in the case of small-
and medium-sized enterprises) and a certain portion of the
training costs are granted for six months. Subsidies are
also granted for employment creation of middle-aged or
older workers in selected depressed areas.

Germany - In Germany, in line with a greater emphasis
on regional concentration of active labour market policies
job creation has been promoted in the sector of social and
community services under a special programme started in
1979 by the federal government for high unemployment
areas. This programme has been created with the twin
objective of a positive employment effect, resulting from
labour-intensive service employment, and the improvement
of the quality of life in the depressed region. The
services sponsored by this scheme include social work for
elderly and disabled persons, care for children of
foreign workers and social counselling. The subsidies
provide for public payment for up to 18 months of 80 per
cent of the wage costs of previously unemployed persons
and for 24 months of 100 per cent of the wage costs for
individuals who had been unemployed for mone than six
months.

Worker Preparation

Our purpose is only to touch the highlights of what
companies and other agencies undertake in order to help
workers be better prepared to shift jobs. In many
countries, the employer of last repose is held account-
able for preparing workers to be in a state of readiness
to enter the labour market.

Even in the United States, where there is no formal
requirement on the part of the discharging employer,
more and more companies have been holding counselling
sessions, hiring consultants, helping workers write
resumés, conducting awareness classes and generally
playing a catalytic role so that the workers are motivated to adopt a positive frame of mind in seeking other
employment. While training sponsored by the "last
employer" has not occurred in the United States as
frequently as in Europe, some companies with enough lead
time have been running in-house training programmes to
help workers get ready for opportunities that exist in
the labour market. For example, Brown and Williamson
has conducted, with the help of the local vocational
school system, skill-broadening sessions for a group of
mechanics whose experience was limited to the cigarette
industry and needed some training so that they could fill
mechanic positions in other companies in Louisville,
Kentucky.

With respect to training, federal funds are available in a number of countries, such as in France, Germany and Sweden, that make it possible for the discharging employer to play a key role in preparing workers for other employment opportunities in the local labour market.

Linkages

A variety of experiences can be cited as "best practice" in this important aspect of re-engagement. Case studies illustrate the wide range of devices that can be utilised to help identify opportunities and to move displaced workers along the right channels.

One large employer in the United States sent out letters to 3,000 employers in a 50-mile radius to help 400 of its displaced workers identify opportunities. In general, a variety of employment-rostering devices have been used to acquaint workers with opportunities in local communities and nearby areas. Some experts in the United States have noted that the single most important variable affecting the overall success of a readjustment effort is the presence of a vital community organisation that can serve as a convening point for the re-employment activities of the local labour market. In Binghampton, New York, a task force that was formed after a large firm closed, established special outreach committees that identified opportunities, worked with the displaced employees, and generally performed a broker function.

In Sweden positive results have been obtained from the co-operation of employment exchange offices, trade unions and enterprises in regard to so-called adjustment groups. In essence this involves a group of persons from the above institutions taking responsibility for the integration into the work process of disadvantaged groups through a flexible planning procedure. There are some 4,500 groups of this nature formed all over Sweden in establishments with more than 50 employees. The functions of the groups are as follows:

- Influencing public opinion as well as the personnel policy of enterprises through information creation and dissemination.
- Measures to promote the recommitment of aged and handicapped workers.
- Use of ergonomists, physicists and psychologists to develop new ideas about adequate work organisation.
- Measures to assist the employed to prepare for promotion.
- Guiding new capital investments in terms of their suitability for employing aged and handicapped workers.

The Swedish experience with these groups in the area of employment of disadvantaged workers could be applied also in the area of work force reduction and job creation.

The possibility of geographical movement is another aspect of creating linkages. In the United States, approxi mately 5 to 10 per cent of a given displaced group usually are willing to move to another geographical area if jobs are in the offing. For example, Brown and Williamson has been able to interest 300 to 400 workers out of a dis- placed group of 3,000 in Louisville to move to Georgia to continue employment with the company. Some years ago, General Foods, in closing down a plant in New England, was able to interest 30 per cent of its workers - many of them white-collar and managerial workers - to move to its new operation in Delaware. The figures for Europe would appear to be substantially lower. One recent example in- volves 40 British workers who had been idled from a Dunlop tyre factory on Merseyside who transferred to another facility of the company in Holland. However, such an example is rare. Geographical mobility is not a very fruitful measure for achieving re-engagement.

Importance of Notice and Consultation

Almost all countries require some period of notice and consultation, except the United States. The advantages of a time period for reckoning, for discussion, for plan- ning, do not need to be elaborated. It would appear that an interval of approximately three months would be ideal, providing a period of time long enough for concrete steps to be planned but not so long as to provide a period of idleness and unproductiveness.

Compensation and Income Protection

One area where the approaches and philosophies appear to differ substantially between countries is income sup- port and other systems of compensation for workers who have been displaced by economic change. We can distinguish between countries such as Britain and the United States where compensation is one of the major elements of the re- adjustment package, and France where it plays a small role in the overall plan for readjustment. Further, we can differentiate between countries where compensation is paid to sever employment arrangements, such as in the United Kingdom, and where compensation is paid to keep a person supported, and attached to the existing employer, as is the case in the United States with the payment of sup- plementary unemployment benefits.

The advantage of presenting an explicit compensation package, as is the case in Britain, is that it induces workers to leave the industry. It would appear that over the past half dozen years, about four times the number of workers have been declared redundant in Great Britain as in the United States. Whereas many workers in the United States have been laid off "subject to recall" and as a result still think of themselves as steelworkers or automobile workers, their chances of recall are very dismal at present. So in this type of situation, the severance or redundancy approach possesses a strong advantage in that it encourages workers to be "bought off" and to look for other work.

On the other side of the ledger, the severance pay approach has the limitation that the money paid is not related to any functional steps that help workers move on to other employment via retraining and/or relocation. During the latter months of the Carter administration, a demonstration project was started in the Detroit area that provided special payments to induce workers to take up retraining, rather than relying solely on unemployment assistance or Trade Adjustment assistance. It is too early to tell what the results of this experiment will be.

Because of the seductive quality of a large "golden handshake" (ranging from £15,000 to £20,000 for some workers who have been recently released from the steel industry in Britain) many people refer to it as "fool's gold". For example, Arthur Scargill, President of the Yorkshire area of the National Union of Mineworkers, recently said that no one has the right to sell off the job opportunities of future generations, and that workers must not fall into the trap of accepting revised payments in exchange for permanent unemployment. Considerable controversy exists over the propriety of large severance payments that induce workers to leave an industry "voluntarily", only to find themselves later in considerable difficulty.

Finally, there is the drawback that once a severance payment programme has been introduced, workers may not be willing to move within the industry, because to do so would be to forego the alternative of a handsome cash settlement. This has been the case in British Steel, where skilled workers are needed in other locations but few will take the transfer because they do not want to forego the large buy-out.

Model Programmes

In this section we would like to consider a number of programmes that tie together the pieces that we have been presenting in this part on labour market re-engagement activities.

Operation by employer - On several occasions we have made mention of a model programme operated by Brown and Williamson. To summarise, the company has put in place a variety of instruments that together add up to a very constructive approach. The company has given 18 months advance notice. Three to four hundred openings in Macon, Georgia, have been earmarked for individuals desiring to transfer from the Louisville facility. For those remaining in Louisville, a variety of retraining efforts and counselling sessions have been instituted. In conjunction with the local vocational education systems, the company has been offering some skill expansion to a group of machinists. Beyond this, several hundred people have completed a high school equivalency programme and have been using the resources of the company to secure other work in the Louisville area. A large group has taken advantage of early retirement, and severance compensation exists for the remainder.

In Japan, employers who are in the structurally depressed industries such as steel manufacturing and shipbuilding must prepare plans concerning assistance to employees governing their re-employment and assist with their job-seeking activities including training allowances. On the other side of the market, employers who hire displacees receive subsidies for six months. Between January 1978 and May 1980, out of the 80,000 persons displaced from selected depressed industries, 50,000 persons have been re-employed through a variety of the measures focusing on the discharging as well as on the receiving employers.(8)

Labour-management efforts - In the case of Portsmouth, Ohio, where a large steel operation closed down recently, a local labour-management group has been working closely with the displaced steelworkers, taking them on trips to Texas (where job openings exist) and serving as a spearhead of activities for the affected workers.

An interesting programme for displaced workers exists in Canada wherein, through the Manpower Consultative Service, several hundred labour-management committees have been established at plants slated to close down, but also in other situations where restructuring of operations (modernisation, expansion, etc.) create a potential for worker dislocation, shortage and retraining. The committees are funded (generally at a level of 50 per cent) by Employment and Immigration Canada. The other half of the funds is provided by the company and the unions. The former normally provides the lion's share. On occasion, provincial governments make a contribution as well.

----

8. Special Group of the Economic Policy Committee on Positive Adjustment Policies, Positive Adjustment Policies: Employment Policy in Japan, OECD, Paris, 31 October 1980.

The Manpower Consultative Service has typically been
applied to situations where the job loss has been gradual.
For sudden large-scale dislocations like the one occurring
in the Canadian auto industry, the government of Canada
has devised the Special Industry and Labour Adjustment
Program which brings together a series of labour adjustment
measures (like portable wage subsidies, training, community
employment development and industry support programmes)
for a more rational application to these special circumstances. Community adjustment committees with representation from business, labour and community organisations
are established under the programme's auspices to foster
and guide the process of economic recovery in the communities where the structural dislocation has had its largest
impact.(9)

Merger of government and private efforts - A very
interesting example of co-operation between government and
private interests comes from "Project 80" wherein the
Swedish shipyards, as they went through merger and restructuring, established a separate organisation to find
permanent employment for approximately 1,600 employees who
were no longer needed in the shipyards. As of March 1980,
almost 35 per cent of this group had acquired other
employment, and an additional 15 per cent had been undergoing training. In addition, another 25 per cent had been
engaged in miscellaneous production, a type of sheltered
workshop arrangement. The work of Project 80 has been
financed through the allocation of state funds.

Some indication of the scale of labour market policy
measures used in Sweden can be gained from the fact that
in the fiscal year 1979-1980 the national labour-market
board's annual budget accounted for 2.5 per cent of the
entire gross national product.(10)

D. JOB CREATION AND REGIONAL DEVELOPMENT

The need for public policies and measures to create
new jobs and to facilitate the economic development of
particular regions arises from uneven structural changes,
leaving major labour market imbalances. Besides regional
and local imbalances in job loss and job creation,
changes may produce imbalances with respect to labour
force groups, occupations and the sex or age composition

---

9. A full description of the Canadian experience is
given in the Dodge Task Force Report on "Labour Market
Development in the 1980s", Employment and Immigration
Canada, 1981.
10. Special Group of the Economic Policy Committee
on Positive Adjustment Policies, Positive Adjustment
Policies in Sweden, OECD, Paris, 16 February 1981.

of employment; the declining and growing job opportunities may have negative impacts on earnings or may deterior-
ate the quality of the job structure in an area.

For the United Kingdom, for example, it has been observed that the displacement component of industrial
development is biased towards manual workers and concentrated in certain regions like the North, Wales, and parts
of the Midlands, through a coincident decline of employment in textiles, iron and steel, coal and railways.
Similarly, job creation has been biased towards non-manual
employment and to regions different from the ones with a
heavy concentration of declining industries. Thus, insurance and banking, fast growing sectors, have been
mainly concentrated in the South-east of Britain.

Labour market imbalances in terms of region, age,
sex and occupation, if they persist, tend to produce reinforcement and consolidation or even deterioration, end-
ing up with difficult problems for plant location, worker
recommitment, and hard-to-employ groups in the labour
force. Very often, we notice major job losses in an
area, followed by a decline in the quality of the local
labour force and erosion of community life.

Such inherent tendencies for aggravation of imbalances and mounting problems for redevelopment may be
regarded as an important argument against "passive"
solutions in the face of significant job loss to an area,
as typified by the out-migration of the young or skilled
segments of the labour force. To keep an area economically viable and attractive for new business, the worsen-
ing of imbalances can be prevented through an active
policy of countering the losses that have occurred and by
strengthening the productive resources available.

Strategic Approaches

A variety of approaches can be distinguished. Some
of the main approaches include public financial incentives
to encourage investment in particular regions of a
country; financial aid to enterprises facing reduction
in employment to encourage them to find alternate products;
creation of jobs by government in the public sector;
subsidies to private firms to create new jobs or to encourage relocation of workers to new jobs; and programmes
initiated and implemented by private firms to create jobs,
using their own financial resources.(11)

---

11. A good overview over the variety of approaches in
several European countries is presented in: Re-examining
European Manpower Policies, A Special Report of the
National Commission for Manpower Policy, No. 10,
Washington, August 1976; and European Labor Market Policies,
A Special Report of the National Commission for Manpower
Policy, Special Report No. 27, Washington, September 1978.

Some of the above categories have already been ana-
lysed. For example, in the section on maintaining the
viability of the business we considered the possibility
of introducing alternative products. Other categories
carry us far beyond the purpose of this paper, for
example, the broad subject of public employment creation
and public relief work. Without going into all of the
reasons, our primary interest here is in the creation of
jobs in the private sector, or at least that sector that
is for the most part considered private, even though in
some countries the industry may be nationalised.

There are two important dimensions within which to
analyse the general subject of job creation and economic
development. The first relates to the target of the programme and whether the emphasis is on creating jobs for
those who have been recently displaced from declining
industries or whether the emphasis is on creating jobs
for those who have been unemployed for a substantial
period of time – the latter involves programmes for dealing with structural unemployment issues in depressed
areas and regions.

The second dimension deals with the impetus, or the
auspices for the job creation, and the source of financial support. Ultimately, the auspices for the creation
of jobs will be the industry, that is, the employer.
Governmental agencies by themselves do not create jobs,
at least in the private sector. However, government can
provide financial assistance and this then becomes the
key distinguishing feature, whether public financial
assistance is channelled to the firm undertaking the job
creation efforts or whether the programme is financed
out of resources available to the enterprise.

In light of all of these distinctions and various
permutations, we would like to concentrate our attention
on two strategic approaches. The first is the well-
established category of regional economic development,
which for the most part is financed by government and
deals with long-term regional problems. The second category involves efforts initiated by enterprises to create
jobs that may be ultimately (and hopefully) filled by
workers that these same enterprises are in the process
of displacing.

Regional Development

In general, looking at the design and application
of these programmes over the past twenty years, we notice
a shift away from general or indiscriminate use of job
creation subsidy schemes. The targeting of job creation
has been induced by increased regional imbalances in the
labour market during the 1970s as well as growing dis-
parities in employment opportunities for different groups
of labour.

While, traditionally, regional subsidies are directed
to the investment of capital, some countries including
Sweden, the United Kingdom, Canada, Austria, Finland,
Italy and Germany added regional subsidies based on the
employment of labour. They are either wage cost subsidies
or grants towards social security costs.

The greater emphasis now placed on employment subsidies instead of grants or other aid to investment of
capital has been caused in part by the increasingly un-
certain or negative employment effects expected from investment schemes. As the share of investment for rationalisation (within the total volume of investment) grows,
the risk increases that the promotion of investment in
high unemployment areas may further contribute to a net
decline in employment as a result of jobs being phased out
in rationalisation efforts and the introduction of more
capital-intensive production methods.

As far as the provision of public support selectively
to particular regions or areas is concerned, there have
been two different approaches to a "regionalisation" of
labour market policy. One is the concentration of public
outlays in areas designated as "problem" or assisted
areas. The other, and sometimes complementary, approach
has been to decentralise the allocation and administration
of regional policy funds.

National approaches - Britain has for a long time
followed a rather generalised approach and has only in
recent years concentrated more on a selective approach to
subsidisation. Successive governments in the 1960s and
1970s have viewed the use of general schemes of governmental financial support and subsidy, including tax incentives, investment grants, regional development grants,
assistance under Section 7 of the Industry Act of 1972 and
the Regional Employment Premiums, as the only practical
way of proceeding on a large scale. It was felt that a
programme aimed at stimulating throughout the country or
towards helping the Assisted Areas could only be taken
in a standardised way. More specific or targeted aid was
given where the government had more specific objectives
in view. Thus, for example, the government brought
forward tailor-made packages of assistance to preserve
the big shipbuilding companies on the Clyde and the
Mersey.(12)

In Sweden, there has also been a tendency to move away
from public employment creation in favour of promoting
more employment in the private sector. In the areas

---

12. G.M. Field and P.B. Hills, "The Administration
of Industrial Subsidies", in: Re-examining European Manpower Policies, op. cit., pp. 207 ff.

affected by the decline of the Swedish shipbuilding industry, regional funds were created. Special regional
aid, regional development funds and regional investment
companies (Swedyard Development Corporation) were established. While the latter was geared towards the creation
of new jobs in the shipyards, the former was directed
towards new employment opportunities in the shipbuilding
regions.

In the case of Germany, one of the programmes for
regional development has been targeted towards areas with
special problems, such as the Ruhr, and is called the
Special Labour Market Programme for Regions with
Particular Employment Problems. This programme calls
for special efforts to stimulate economic restructuring
and to create new employment opportunities in problem
areas, with the Ruhr being a primary example. Thus, in
the case of Germany, a regional disparity in the func-
tioning of the labour markets has been answered by policies that seek to deal with some of the underlying problems facing different labour markets.

For France, an example of regional development comes
out of the much cited experience with Lorraine. As a
part of helping the area (which during the late 1970s
lost approximately 15,000 steel jobs), the government
came forward with an industrial adaptation fund of
approximately $700 million. This money has been used to
pay half the capital cost and also to provide interest-
free loans for new factories being constructed in the
Lorraine area. Emphasis has also been placed on using
the money on a per-job basis and approximately $6,000
can be granted for each job created in the target area.

Job Creation Efforts by Enterprises

In the United Kingdom, the British Steel Corporation (BSC) has taken the responsibility to develop or
assist new job opportunities in areas affected by major
plant closures. BSC's commercial and marketing network
is used for finding companies looking for industrial
development sites. Starting in 1975, British Steel
focused its job creation efforts through a new subsidiary
called British Steel Corporation Industries which had as
its main purpose "to bring jobs to areas of the country
where steel plants are being closed". Under the programme, BSC Industries does not provide direct financial
assistance to firms in the steel-making areas, but uses
its "good offices" to focus financial assistance from
other sources such as the government, the Common Market
and financial institutions. BSC Industries sees itself
as a broker, a catalyst, a stimulator of interest and a
provider of technical assistance. Furthermore, BSC
Industries attempts to apply its own relatively diverse

product range, its internal product development and its R & D programmes to the creation of job opportunities in areas affected by closures - either directly or indirectly through joint ventures. Ebbw Vale represents one example where BSC Industries established two job-creating projects and, also, persuaded one of its major suppliers to site its expansion in an area hit by closures.(13)

One concept that has been pioneered is that of the "neighbourhood workshop". BSC Industries has found space in buildings that might have otherwise been demolished and has made available facilities for a range of small businesses. For example, in the Rollcross area, over 54 small companies employing approximately 400 people moved into one of these buildings. Most of the businesses were new and were taking advantage of the space and the packaging help provided by BSC Industries. In terms of overall results, by the end of 1979 approximately 2,400 jobs had been created and BSC Industries estimated that by early 1982 another 5,000 jobs would be created.

Given the extensive amount of job loss and worker displacement in the United Kingdom, it is not surprising that a number of other companies, usually large scale, have instituted job creation efforts in areas where oper-ations are being terminated. For example, Tate and Lyle has put in motion a job creation plan which puts the company in the role of a merchant banker. The company will invest between £10,000 and £20,000 per job created in businesses that have good financial prospects and where the enterprises will give the employees being dis-placed from Tate and Lyle "first refusal". An example of this approach is the investing by Tate and Lyle of approximately £400,000 for the prospect of creating 150 jobs in the Port Glasgow area.(14)

Massey Ferguson has used an industry search firm to forward over 1,000 letters to chambres of commerce and banks alerting them to the availability of space in its Kilmarnock facility where approximately 1,500 workers became redundant in early 1980. As of the time of the report, it was too early to tell whether any large firm or series of small firms would be interested in using the space owned by the company.(14)

Another example comes from the North-west area of Britain which has been hard hit by redundancies over the past several years. During the mid-1970s extensive cut-backs took place at Pilkington. Realising that large

---

13. John Hughes, "Industrial Restructuring: Some Manpower Aspects", National Economic Development Office, Discussion Paper 4, 1976, pp. 37-38.
14. Industrial Relations Review and Report, January 1980, p. 2.

companies and other economic interest groups could do something to enhance the long-run viability of the area, a number of business leaders came together in 1979 to form St. Helen's Trust with the largest backing coming from Pilkington in the amount of £50,000.

The Trust operates in a number of ways: first, it will finance new businesses with small loans, second, it will provide professional advice and training and finally, it will "run interference" with various government agencies in handling the red tape associated with getting new enterprises underway. In the first year and a half of operation, approximately 500 full-time and 200 part-time jobs were created in the area.

Perhaps the most ambitious programme undertaken by a private firm in France is the efforts of Rhône-Poulenc which, through its subsidiary Sopran, has created about 700 jobs to help fill the gap created by some 3,000 displaced workers made redundant as a result of the company closing down a number of its nylon and polyester fibre operations. Sopran offers financial resources to a new company as well as providing building and transportation facilities. It has also been able to entice firms to take up location near some of its ongoing facilities where products are complementary.(15)

Evaluation

A full-fledged evaluation of various regional development policies and programmes is not a matter on which we would claim comparative advantage, nor is it really part of the main focus of this paper. In attempting to assess whether regional development policies represent "good practice" one would need to take account of gross and net employment effects, displacement effects and other macroeconomic relationships. Nevertheless, a few comments in passing can be made about the two categories that we have given attention to in this section.

Regional economic development - Based on a range of evidence, it is our conclusion that regional economic development policies do not help directly (at least in the first instance) workers being displaced from their places of employment. Typically, what happens when new jobs are created in a region is that they go to younger workers in the labour market or to others who transfer into the area to take advantage of the new opportunities. The middle-aged and older workers, who often represent the bulk of those displaced, usually fill other positions in the labour market that might be vacant, creating a type of secondary effect or benefit.

---

15. Chemical Week, 10 January 1979.

Another consideration is that jobs created in a
regional economic development programme may not represent
long-term jobs. There is some evidence, especially from
development areas in Scotland, that firms view the inducements to locate in an area and to create jobs as a
type of asset which they deplete over a period of 5 to 10
years. At the end of this time period they "pick up
stakes" and move on to some other development area to
capture a new set of inducements. These points are specu-
lative, however, and we had better rest with the beginning
point of the section, that the full evaluation of regional
development policies should be left to the experts.

Job creation by enterprises - Certainly, it should be
clear that the number of jobs created in the examples we
have given represents only a small fraction of the workers
being displaced. It is just a fact of economic life that
the small businesses, which tend to be the focus for job
creation efforts, do not generate many jobs. This is despite the assertion that "Small is Beautiful" and the substantial interest that the subject of entrepreneurship
and small business development has received over the past
several years.

A further factor is that not too many of the workers
being displaced benefit from new jobs created directly or
indirectly by their former employer. The closer the
linkage between the displacee and the new job, the better
the chance of a match. If the new job is created by the
same employer, represents the same occupation and at the
same location, then the gap is not great and there is a
good chance that the workers will gravitate to the new
positions. However, introduce a new employer (who would
like to hire the best people available in the labour
market) or the requirement that the displaced workers have
to move to another section of the labour market (not to
mention moving to another section of the country) or the
fact that the work is different and requires retraining,
then the chances of the new jobs benefitting the displacees become exceedingly small.

Maintaining a balanced perspective or realising that
the glass is half-full and half-empty - Two areas that
have been hit very hard by cutbacks in the steel industry - Corby (Britain) and Lorraine (France) - illustrate
the very mixed picture that regional economic development
presents. Consider some of the general statistics for
Corby. This is a town with approximately 55,000 in-
habitants, wherein British Steel has cut back employment
by 6,000 workers (with approximately 5,000 remaining
employed). Most of the workers who have been displaced
from the steel industry, even though they originally came
from Scotland, have remained in Corby anticipating that
jobs will develop to fill the vacuum.

92

The Corby Development Corporation along with BSC Industries and the government have moved ahead with a variety of programmes to fill the gap created by the extensive cutbacks at BSC Industries. The corporation estimates that to create jobs for the displacees would take land and factories and substantial new investments. The area has been designated as a Development Area by the government, which should give it an edge in attracting new industry. Also, money is available from the European Coal and Steel Community to help with vocational training for those who are changing career lines. The positive view is that Corby, because of its location, will attract industry. One example of this is that Oxford University Press will move one of its main distribution operations into Corby, eventually employing some 200 people. On the other side is the point of view that Corby will never return to its previous level of employment. Workers and their families will have to move out of Corby into other areas, primarily the South-east of Britain, where more growth is taking place.

A similar mixed picture can be derived from the Lorraine region where even larger cutbacks have taken place in steel employment. The French government planned to induce automobile companies to expand production in Lorraine; but due to the fall off in demand for automobiles, this programme has been modified substantially. Some jobs have been added to the area, but many of the workers have remained unemployed on a long-term basis.

How an area fares over the long term after experiencing substantial work force displacements depends on many factors, of which the relative size of the cutbacks is particularly important. We know of one instance where the cutback actually produced a positive shock effect on the economic development of the area. The lay-offs were large enough to catch everyone's attention and to mobilise special programmes, but not so large that the challenge could not be met.

VI

PATTERNS OF CHANGE AND RESPONSE

In this chapter we start the task of drawing together
some of the patterns that describe the process of economic
restructuring, as it is performed in a variety of industries and countries. In the first section we examine some
of the patterns that can be best understood by reference
to the nature of the economic restructuring that is taking
place. Then we move to consider some of the relationships that appear to be characteristic of the adjustment
cycle itself. Finally, we would like to draw some comparison across countries and industries and to examine
various strategies of change and relate these to the
results.

THE PRECIPITATING PRESSURES

We can distinguish different types of forces that
drive industries into some type of economic restructuring.
First, there is the category of a sharp fall-off in
demand: a situation characteristic of many industries
today that suffer from over-capacity. Second, there can
be a fundamental change in the nature of the products and/
or technologies being employed - requiring some rapid
adjustments to new modes of production. Finally, there is
the classic problem of competitive pressures or high-cost
operations that forces enterprises into a series of coping
techniques in order to preserve market shares.

Drop in demand - This economic attribute characterises a number of industries today and for several of them
it is occurring on a worldwide basis. For example, shipbuilding activity has fallen off in every industrialised
country. While the steel industry is not down in every
country, it is down on an overall basis and for a number
of countries (all of those in our survey) sharp cutbacks
in operating rates have occurred.

One strategy that has been followed in a number of situations to deal with excess capacity is the shrinking of the industry via consolidation and mergers. For example, this approach has been followed in Sweden in both the shipbuilding and steel sectors. In fact, generally speaking, this approach appears to have been the main response on the part of most countries to the plight of their shipbuilding industries.

In retrospect, it is not clear that the consolidation strategy has proved effective, given the size of the contraction that has been required. Merger and consolidation activities consume considerable time and effort and it might have been as effective to have eliminated large segments of the industry and allowed new and more efficient elements to develop "de novo". (We will return to the question whether a viable sector can be created more readily from segments of the existing industry or whether the best chances are with new ventures and new enterprises that emerge outside the established traditions and arrangements of the existing industry.)

The difficult task facing the parties and their governments is how to come down the "slippery slopes of decline" without too much disruption and turmoil for the workers and the communities involved. Generally speaking, the approach that has been taken has been to use attrition and other human resource devices to absorb the excess workers, especially during the early phases of the crisis. However, as the crisis has deepened it has become necessary to sever workers. In this phase a variety of readjustment arrangements have been used, such as Project 80 (a type of sheltered employment), as well as transfer to other enterprises as has been the case in Japan.

Given the depth of the crisis in shipbuilding, governments have had to play a role, especially to help in the cushioning of the severe impact that such a sharp fall-off in economic activity has provoked. The unions for their part have been generally co-operative, especially in the early phases of retrenchment. However, as the crisis has deepened and it has become clearer that the industry is in a "no win" situation for the workers, the unions have moved into either a defensive or an aloof posture. For example, some of the unions in British shipbuilding have not been willing to join in discussions about further decline in that industry. In the case of Sweden, the unions first "looked the other way" and more recently have taken a harder line to further cutbacks. In the next chapter we will examine the very delicate role that union leaders are placed in as industry proceeds down the steep slopes of decline.

Changes in product and technology - This economic circumstance describes much of what has happened in the rubber industry, as well as in a large part of the automobile industry — not to mention a variety of other industries that have adopted new technologies and new modes of production. In most instances, new technology is labour saving — indeed, it is via this avenue that increases in productivity have occurred historically. The question of interest to this study is whether the pace and the nature of the technological change is such as to create large numbers of excess workers. In most instances, technological change, per se, does not create large-scale displacement. However, in the past some instances have occurred: and no doubt as the revolution of the "chip" continues to run its course, there will be other such groups of displacees.

One interesting illustration of the impact of the pace of change is the textile industry. Employment in this industry, for most industrialised countries, has been sharply affected by increases in productivity: in fact, employment has been affected more from this source than from imports. Several countries have moved aggressively to encourage their textile industries to scrap outmoded equipment and this has produced a substantial displacement of workers in the industries. Japan seems to have followed this policy quite vigorously. However, the programme in the United Kingdom, operated in the 1960s, was not as successful. Thus, in the short run, the displacement of labour was not as great as ultimately desired, since the industry remained more labour intensive than it could afford over the long run — given competitive pressures from the development of modern operations in other countries, more displacement sooner might have forestalled even greater displacement later.

A situation where displacement is generated by new technology lends itself admirably to the human resource management approach, especially since a new technology usually requires the transformation of the skill base of a work force. In fact, some examples exist where industries over a period of time have adopted new technologies and have used a range of training programmes — as a result they have been able to adapt their existing work force to dramatically different technologies. The telephone industry certainly fits this description. Also, some of the developments in the automobile industry around the world, as robots and sophisticated electronics have been introduced, also fall into this category.

While many companies have developed the skills required by retraining their existing workers, others have used new workers for new methods: for example, where the new products and new technology require the erection of new plants, perhaps in new areas of the country, as has happened with radial tyre plants in the United States. Then the existing work force does not benefit from the changes, and we see a side-by-side phasing out of old plants (with readjustment programmes to move workers to

new industries in the same areas) and the development of
sophisticated training programmes in "sunbelt" areas of
the United States to train workers to handle the new
technology involved in the new tyre plants. This example
is probably somewhat unique to the United States given
the intra-country mobility patterns of industry and does
not characterise as much the European Members of OECD.

High cost operations - This factor describes a number of industries and is often present with some other
economic pressures. The steel industry in the United
States, United Kingdom, France, as well as several other
countries, suffers from being high cost. The strategy
that is appropriate for dealing with high cost operations
is some form of productivity bargaining or rollback of
benefits - i.e. some programme that labour and management
"hammer out", coming to grips with the lack of competitiveness in the operations.

It is in these circumstances that the parties can be
constructive and aggressive and move to eliminate the
"fat", in order for the remaining operation to be as
competitive and as viable as possible. The United Steelworkers of America have recently adopted a more aggressive
stance to help solve some of the high cost problems of
their industry. Unlike a crisis stemming from a drop in
world demand, there is a chance, in this context, for the
enterprise or industry to hold its market share, if some
of the underlying competitive problems can be solved.
Hence, union leaders have something positive to deliver
to their members: enhanced job security.

THE ADJUSTMENT CYCLE

In discussing the shipbuilding industry in the preceding section, we alluded to the fact that the crisis
often runs through some type of cycle wherein the problems "seem to get worse before they get better". At
this point we would like to generalise about this
phenomenon and introduce the concept of the "S" curve,
which is similar to the learning curve that has appeared
in many pieces of literature about the introduction of
new ideas and the diffusion of innovations.

When we use the concept of the "S" curve, we are
describing on one axis the needed displacement of workers
versus time on the other. This concept implies that for
the early stages of the crisis the needed displacement
of workers may be small; then as the crisis deepends,
the number of workers who should be displaced grows
quite rapidly and finally, as the crisis ends, the displacement activity ends and the industry once again finds
itself in equilibrium. We would contend that this "S"

curve describes the first form of economic pressure, namely, a drop in world demand. The configuration also describes a surge of new technology, since typically there is a period of tentative introduction, that is, trial and error: it is during this period that many firms watch the initiators. As the technology becomes stabilised, a rush to introduce it takes place: it is at this point in the cycle that the potential displacement of workers is greatest.

A good illustration of the "S" curve in operation is the textile industry in the United States over the past 15 or 20 years. Between 1963 and 1970 employment was declining about 0.5 per cent per year, then it moved to 1 per cent per year for the years 1970 to 1973 and for the period 1973 to 1980, it reached almost 3 per cent per year. So it would appear that for this industry we have recently been witnessing the steep portion of the "S" curve. It can be anticipated within the next 5 or 10 years that the adjustment cycle would be over and the displacement rate would have dropped back to near-normal levels.

A major complicating factor in this form of analysis is in making a prediction whether an industry is entering into an adjustment cycle or whether it is just going through a cyclical fall-off in demand, soon to be followed by a restoration of markets. It is always easier to analyse the data ex post, as in the case of the textile industry; it is another to do it ex ante for an industry that is entering into some type of downturn.

Hindsight underscores the costs that come from delay: but there are also costs from closing down facilities and displacing workers if demand will return in the near future. For example, Ford Motor of Canada and Brown and Williamson in the United States, have both been cutting back on facilities and helping place workers in the local labour market, only to find out that demand (in these two situations) has come back much more strongly than anticipated. As a result the companies have had to recall workers from other employment and to suffer poor public relations with other employers in the local communities, who co-operated with the readjustment programmes only to find that many of their new workers were attracted back to the companies that erroneously appeared to be in decline.

Some help in sorting out whether the displacement is likely to be permanent or not can come from the earlier analysis as to the type of economic pressure that is present. If the basic problem is one of high cost or introduction of new technology, the displacement is likely to be permanent. The only category where there may be some doubt is the first category, "fall-off in demand".(1)

It is precisely in decline-in-demand situations where potentially large-scale displacements are involved; yet it is in such circumstances where the parties are often most "in the dark" as to whether the decline is short or long term. Typically what happens is that the parties embark upon some type of human resource management - and for the early phases of the crisis this is usually sufficient. It is also the case that attrition rates are higher, or can be induced to be higher, during the early phases of the crisis. Consequently, some match occurs between the techniques for handling excess workers and the early slope of the "S" curve that does not require too many workers to be displaced.

Subsequently, a type of scissors effect often develops as natural or induced attrition drops (those who can be retired early have departed) and, if at the same time the crisis deepends, the need for potential displacement also increases. This is the critical phase which can be illustrated for several industries. For example, in the early phases of the retrenchment for British Steel, workers were retired and displaced on a gradual basis. This came to be called the era of "change with a human face" and experts commented quite positively about the changes that were being made to cut back on capacity and the way in which it was being handled in a very sensible fashion with respect to the workers involved. However, that was the early 1970s. Today the industry is in such dire straits and the cutbacks so substantial that no one is talking about human resource management programmes.

Similarly, the contrasting approaches taken at different points in the cycle over the past 20 years in Swedish shipbuilding provide a good illustration of the sequencing of different policies in line with altered market outlooks. As long as the difficulties were believed to be temporary, a reconsolidation approach through mergers and rationalisation predominated. Thereafter, as the long-term business prospects turned worse, a planned attrition approach with the aim of avoiding lay-offs was organised. In the latest phase of adjustment, a plan of

---

1. We should also note that when technological change or high cost pressures are the driving force, then the potential displacement is usually steady and can be phased into digestible groups of workers. Indeed, human resource management plays a very key role in planning and implementing programmes for handling those who are no longer needed as a result of introduction of new technology or the improvement of productivity to deal with high-cost operations.

reorientation of the shipbuilding industry towards closing down facilities and developing new products and new markets has come to the fore.

In closing this section, we might take note of hindsight and underscore a dilemma that is faced by the parties at the point of cross-over, or what we have called the scissors effect. It is precisely at this point in the unfolding of the adjustment cycle that the parties have in some instances backed off from further change, because of the extreme social consequences of declaring people redundant or, in one way or another, moving them out of the industry of their employment. In a number of situations, then, the day of reckoning has been delayed, only to return with more severe consequences at some future point. For example, the substantial adjustment currently taking place in British coalmining and steel can in part be traced to the inability of the parties in the mid-1970s to continue the process of "shedding labour". The same point can be made about the recent difficulties in the French steel industry in the Lorraine district.

In defence of how these situations have been handled, it can be said that the parties genuinely believed that times would get better and that they had done a heroic job of cutting back on employment and modernising the industries. Nonetheless, these industries stopped too early in the readjustment cycle - probably because the workers and the communities that would be potentially affected were able to stop the process of transition through political means. If producers succeed in securing the support of governments, there is no chance of carrying the economic changes through until the crisis develops to the point where the public says "enough is enough" and forces the restructuring process to continue.

STRATEGIES AND RESULTS

We would like to pick up a number of summary points about overall strategies and what seems to work and not to work.

1. In a number of important instances the vital elements that emerge in the process of economic restructuring appear to be outside the established sector of the industry. For example, the breakthrough in Italian textiles has come from the smaller firms that have not been helped by the government, and not from the large firms in the established sector. In the United States the fastest growing segment of the steel industry is the "minimills" that are being constructed, often in the sunbelt, and very close to the growing markets. Usually they are not unionised. Some of the same points could

be made about the growth of this element of the Italian steel industry.

Another illustration (also from the United States) is the experience of the meat-packing industry, which was the subject of many surveys and projects in the 1950s (for example the Armour Automation Committee). It appears that the major companies such as Armour and Swift have abandoned the business of meat packing. The market has been taken over by a new "breed" of companies that have moved closer to the source of supply, have established modern facilities and often operate on a non-union basis.

2. On the other hand, we can cite several examples where, in the established sector, the large companies have taken the lead and have been the force for re-vitalising the industry. For example, in France a number of large dynamic and aggressive textile companies have acquired many smaller firms, thereby improving their overall line of product.

The same point could be made with respect to a number of large United States textile firms which have been prospering. They have introduced new technology, they have taken advantage of lower cost operations in the South and some of the economies coming from long runs. As a result they have been steadily capturing a larger and larger share of world markets. Thus, the picture of reindustrialisation is mixed as to whether the innovations and new currents are occurring primarily outside or within established sectors. It would take an economic historian to understand this contrast but superficially we feel the explanation rests with an analysis of the entrepreneurial spirit which appears to be so necessary to achieve some type of breakthrough. The entrepreneurial spirit applies to both the conception (that is the new idea concerning products and ways of organising to produce those products) and a certain toughness to change the established ways and to persevere against the inherent resistance to change. The extent to which this entrepreneurial spirit exists within established groups or the extent to which it needs to find this expression in breaking out of old moulds is an interesting subject to contemplate. The United States would seem to favour the first mode, whereas in Germany and Japan there seems to be an entrepreneurial spirit within established firms to identify new markets, to tailor the organisations to meet these new markets and to move ahead in a steady and determined way to tap these opportunities.

3. Finally, we would like to turn to the employment side of the strategic question. One conclusion that emerges from examination of a wide variety of adjustment programmes is that the commitment to handle the employment consequences of economic change needs to rest at the highest levels of management. The firms that appear

most successful in integrating "the economic must with the human ought" are those that factor employment consider-ations into long-run business planning and actually reconcile the tensions between the capital and labour sides of the business on a strategic basis. A number of "high-tech" firms that operate worldwide have maintained continuity of employment, thereby eliminating some of the problems that we have considered in this monograph, by asking themselves, when they are embarking upon new business ventures: What are the employment consequences and will the firm be able to sustain its commitment to the workers over the long term as a result of undertaking this project? This integration has been developed to its best refinement within Japan, especially for the side of the economy emphasizing career employment.

Such a commitment to continuity of employment for the existing work force means that, as economic change occurs, ways will be found to retain and redeploy existing workers. The location of employment may change but workers can count on opportunities to work with the same firm. Such an approach can only work where the growing segments of the business can be tapped by the same firms that are experiencing decline. This describes large firms which are able to keep abreast of economic developments. It certainly does not apply to the development of new firms such as the minimills in the steel industry. The workers who come into these enter-prises come from other sectors, often rural occupations; and those who have worked in the large basic steel companies are not the ones making the changeover.

4. Certainly, in many situations the changes in the environment are such (perhaps becaue of a sharp fall-off in demand) that the work force cannot be accommodated to the lines of business that are available. This provokes a crisis: a situation of excess labour. The factor of potential excess labour should not stop the introduction of new technology, nor the elimination of high-cost operations. The question is how to deal with the excess – we have been discussing a variety of techniques that range from human resource planning, to lay-off coupled with readjustment programmes that help workers find other employment.

In passing, we might note that there have been many instances, in many industries and many countries, in which the potential of excess employment has stopped economic change: as a result, not only are the workers initially at risk excess, but over the long run many more workers become excess, because a "remaining core" has not been achieved that can be competitive and can make it in work markets. The concept used in Sweden of Project 80, wherein the excess workers are transferred away from the main enterprise and held in a sheltered arrangement, makes very good sense. This is far superior to keeping the excess workers in the enterprise as has been done on the United States railroads and in many newspapers in the United States and in the United Kingdom.

THE STEEL INDUSTRY AS A MICROCOSM OF THE ADJUSTMENT CYCLE

The steel industry serves as a very good vehicle for summarising a number of points that we have been making about the nature of the underlying economic pressures, the adjustment strategies undertaken, and the results achieved.

The nature of the economic problem - The countries that seem to have experienced the most difficulty with their steel industries, the United Kingdom and France, are characterised by a history in which the industries emphasized bulk steel in contrast to a greater development of "know how" and technologies for speciality products. The philosophy of "big is beautiful" imbued the thinking of top management in British Steel, and to some extent the counterpart companies in France. (In the latter case, a key decision was made in the 1960s to expand employment and capacity of the steel industry in Lorraine.) Thus, the steel industries in these two countries not only face the general problem of the steel industry around the world, namely, decline in demand, but they face a particular problem since their capacity for bulk steel is greater: it is this part of the market that has been dropping most drastically.

Response patterns - In terms of response, a number of companies have pursued the merger and restructuring route. For example, in the United States, Youngstown Sheet and Tube was acquired by a conglomerate. In the case of Sweden, the steel companies have been merged. The question to be asked is whether mergers will solve any of the basic problems. Does putting weak parts together create anything more than a weak merger?

The best response pattern appears to have taken place in Germany, where the restructuring programme has emphasized specialty steels and has involved a substantial amount of retraining of the work forces to exploit new opportunities. Another strategy which has been employed successfully is the introduction of sophisticated new technologies. The productivity advantage of new technologies and new plants is perhaps of the order of four times as great as that existing in the older facilities. Consequently, a firm cannot remain in the market place without moving to modern technology.

In terms of coping with excess capacity, aside from
the point that "sooner is better", one approach that
appears to be associated with success is the following:
surgery to weed out the old plants and to take the cuts
in a specified way rather than reducing operations across
the board. Hence, Nippon Steel closed down an entire
mill complex; similarly, British Steel is closing down a
number of inland facilities. The same pattern of adjustment describes the United States, where major cuts have
come in the Buffalo and Youngstown areas.

Japan appears to have a long view and to understand
the life cycle of an industry such as steel. It is
reported that the Japanese see themselves moving out of
some aspects of the steel industry, in recognition of the
cost advantage that other countries such as Korea and
Taiwan will possess in the future. The Japanese example
illustrates how planning by the firm coupled with help
from government can anticipate changes at early stages,
thereby initiating the adjustment in timely fashion.

Role of government - It would appear that the best
results have come where government remains in the background and where management has taken the initiative to
fashion a restructuring solution. This would describe
the approach in Germany. However, in the case of Japan
the government has played a more direct role, although it
is still a minor partner. This pattern is perhaps a clue
to the balance to be achieved. Where the industry has
been owned or dominated by government, as in Britain,
Sweden and France, the economic difficulties of the steel
industries seem to be much greater.

Readjustment approaches - As far as the out-placement
of excess workers is concerned, the German and Japanese
experiences of emphasizing early retirement and transfer
to other work within the control of the conglomerate seems
to represent very effective strategies. By contrast, the
approach taken in the United States of laying off workers
and providing continuing support via unemployment insurance and trade adjustment assistance does not represent positive practice because there is little redeployment of workers. Indeed, the workers continue to
think of themselves as steelworkers; they remain in
the communities; and they hope for the improbable event
of being recalled to their former plants.

COUNTRIES WITH THE BEST PRACTICE:
GERMANY AND JAPAN

Since many of the examples of integrative adjustment
come from these two countries, a few more words should be
said at this point about the conditions which have

facilitated better results. As we have noted, in these countries the economic adjustment process has started sooner rather than later, and workers have been accommodated in reasonably effective fashion.

What explains these better results? The first explanation lies in the industrial structure of these countries. Businesses in the affected industries tend to be large and multi-industry in character. This has made it possible for redeployment to take place under the auspices of the large firm, for example the movement of workers from the steel to the automobile sectors of a large Japanese conglomerate. Second, management generally has believed in the value of sharing information and involving unions, either through the structure of co-determination or through more informal processes of consultation.

The unions, for their part, have tended to take a constructive view of economic change and have recognised the importance of getting on with reindustrialisation in order to preserve industry's position in various export markets. The workers themselves have been much more "export-minded" than their counterparts in other countries such as Britain and the United States.

The geographical dispersion and organisation of industry has also made it possible for workers to change employment without changing residential areas. Thus, the location of the steel industry in Germany and Japan, in their industrial heartlands, unlike its more remote location in the United States, the United Kingdom and France, has made it possible for steelworkers to be more readily redeployed.

Finally, the institutions and traditions of the countries with respect to training and instilling new skills to keep abreast of new technology have also facilitated the adjustment process. It is here where the respective governments play a very important role in helping to finance and guide the training and readjustment processes.

VII

In this chapter we examine some critical features of
the process itself and the extent to which workers and
their union representatives are involved. The question is
whether the adjustment process takes place strictly as a
management undertaking, or whether there is substantial
participation on the part of workers and their representatives. This can be portrayed within a dimension ranging
from unilateral to multilateral decision-making.

Unilateral versus multilateral decision-making -
This dimension refers to the number and kind of actors or
groups involved in developing and implementing dislocation
policies at the various levels of decision-making; more
specifically, how far and in what ways are firms or
management, unions (or worker representatives) and governments involved in finding and executing solutions? The
participation of actors in decision-making will be one
major determining factor on the outcomes, in terms of the
sharing of costs and burdens to various parties involved.
Thus, management may try to maintain discretion over
structural change and adjustment; or more co-operative
solutions and procedures may be involved.

THE PHILOSOPHICAL ORIENTATION OF WORKERS
AND UNIONS TOWARDS PARTICIPATION

On the one hand, a minority of unions do not want to
be involved in any aspect of economic restructuring and
the related processes of worker readjustment. The
following kind of statement is made by some union
leaders: "It is management's job to do the business of
running the enterprise". Union leaders are understandably
weary of getting involved in a process when the "news is
all bad". Off the record, some of them confide that
unions getting involved only slows down the process of
change, with the possible result that the job security
of the "remainder" becomes even more insecure. Hence,

some union leaders, without openly saying it, prefer
management to take the initiative and to push ahead "with
all deliberate speed". This perspective suggests that
union leaders "look the other way" at times of economic
crises.

While not too many leaders fall into the "aloof"
category, there is a tendency for more of them to shift to
this mode as the crisis deepens - that is, as the later
and more critical stages of retrenchment are experienced,
in terms of the cycle of readjustment. As we mentioned
earlier, withdrawal by union leaders has occurred in the
case of the Swedish shipyards as they have proceeded
through successive cutback programmes in dealing with a
chronic over-capacity situation.

The predicament of participation - Helping to shape
business decisions presents an acute predicament for
union leaders and worker representatives. They find themselves in a dilemma, with sharply drawn disadvantages on
each side. On the one hand, if they become involved,
they may be viewed by the rank and file as having been
co-opted by management and thereby suffer the stigma
associated with business demise. These fears are well
illustrated by the experience of some of the unions in
British Steel who have been blamed by rank and file members
and community representatives for having gone along with
the decisions that have dismantled a large part of the
steel-making capacity. Worker directors, who have been
"associated" with the decisions, have been treated as
strangers in their home communities.

On the other hand, if union leaders do not get involved to challenge the business decision they will also
be condemned; an illustration comes from the United
States. The United Automobile Workers represented
approximately 1,000 workers at a Dana Corporation plant
in Wisconsin making front-end axles. In a survey conducted among the workers about a year after the plant
closed down, the workers expressed many more negative
feelings about the union than about management. The
workers viewed management as having made an inevitable
decision to close the plant down in the face of a drop
in demand that hit the recreational-vehicle industry.
However, the workers felt that the union should have done
more to force the company to transfer other work into the
plant or to have put pressure on the company to close
another plant. Union representatives are seen as having
failed in their tasks, since it is their responsibility
to make job security the number-one objective. If job
security is not pressed, there can be a substantial back-
lash against union leaders.

Thus far, we have been considering the outlook of
national union leaders. If we introduce local union
leaders into the discussion, the interest in participation

107

takes a different turn. Let us differentiate national
from local union leadership along two dimensions:
economic understanding and economic stakes. With respect
to the first variable, the extent of sophistication regarding the "economic facts of life", the national union
leadership has the best record and probably understands
better the life cycle of decline and what is really in the
offing in the industry. Thus, in an informational sense,
national leaders have the strongest reason to get involved. On the other hand, they may not stand to gain by
getting involved, because the changes need to take place
anyway and the overall position of union strength may not
be altered by whether they are involved or not. This
point of view has affected the thinking of many union
leaders in the United States who know that the companies
will be establishing modern plants in new areas of the
country (hopefully, under union contract): it may not
make a great deal of difference to the central union
leadership whether they represent workers in established
urban areas or in new sunbelt areas.

By contrast, workers at the local level are much
more apt to be concerned about the shape of the change:
their desire to be involved stems from a need to protect
their own position.

If we conceptualise and describe the variables as
willingness to get involved as the crisis deepens, versus
the interest in making concessions to save jobs, we derive
the following diagram. As the crisis deepens the
national leadership is less likely to join the issue
because it is a "no win" situation for them, whereas the
rank and file are more interested in getting involved to
make concessions and to explore ways of saving the operation.

Trend of growing involvement - Despite the reluctance
of some labour leaders (limited desirability) and despite
the difficulty of labour leaders gaining access (limited
feasibility), more and more leaders appear to be interested and involved in the process of economic change.
For example, leaders of the unions in the shipbuilding
industry in Japan have committed themselves to greater
involvement in the rationalisation efforts going on in
the shipyards.

Even in the United States, where unions have more
times than not taken the first view of aloofness, there
is growing evidence that unions are becoming more involved in the subject of economic restructuring. Without
the involvement of the United Autoworkers and Doug Fraser
on the Board of Chrysler, it is unlikely that the company
would have been saved, that the concessions of substantial
proportions would have been put through (thereby reducing labour costs by $600 million) and that the enter-
prise (without substantial restructuring) would have been
placed on a viable basis for the long run.

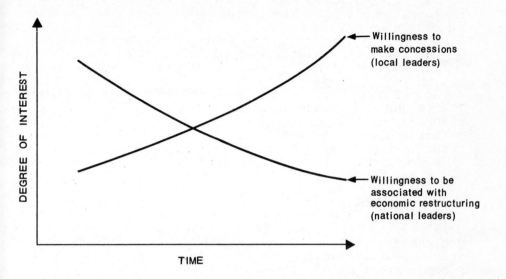

Further, as a result of the United Autoworkers'
involvement in Chrysler, a committee has been established
that will look at the shutdown of plants. As Fraser has
said, "We can move on the decision before it becomes irreversible and the committee can consider alternatives,
such as finding other uses for the plant, farming out the
excess capacity to others, and exploring the prospects
for workers purchasing the plant and possibly setting up
programmes for retraining of workers".(1) Fraser credits
the committee with scheduling more work for a glass plant
instead of closing it down and keeping open four other
plants in the Detroit area.(2)

Similarly, the Steelworkers' Union in the United
States, which has heretofore taken a very distant attitude with respect to business decisions, has become much
more involved in monitoring the maintenance and capital
budgeting decisions of the large steel companies. The
union realises that the jobs of their members are at
stake and they are evidencing, although tentatively, a
new involvement in this area.

1. New York Times, 31 August 1980, p. 19.
2. Wall Street Journal, 12 March 1981.

Similarly, in Britain, where unions traditionally have also tended to stay aloof of any involvement in managerial decisions, there has been some reorientation lately on the national level. Representatives of the TUC and CBI have agreed in principle on the text of a joint statement on new technology covering, among other things, decision-making about technological change, including the provision of information to workers' representatives, prior consultation and joint machinery for examining planned technological changes; the implementation of technological change and its impact on security of employment, manpower planning, skills, training and retraining, company competitiveness and growth. The statement recognises the need for rapid technological change and points out that this would most likely be achieved on the basis of a joint approach.(3)

The involvement of unions and workers in economic restructuring and worker displacement has probably been developed to the greatest degree in Germany, and it is desirable at this point to enumerate the various forms in which co-determination and union involvement have taken place in that country.

At the micro level, this co-operative-type exchange relationship is carried on within the institutional framework of co-determination. It involves communication with, consultation with and co-determination by the works council in such matters as personnel planning, working conditions and work force reduction. As part of their representation on the supervisory boards of corporations, employees and trade unions take part directly in crucial decision-making, including investment decisions.

At the supra-enterprise level employers, trade unions, the federal and state governments and communities are represented on the Board of the Federal Employment Institute, a self-governing body incorporated under public law and entrusted with the execution and administration of public manpower policy. This participation takes place in the national head office as well as in 9 regional and 146 local employment offices.

With regard to industrial and general economic policy, there has been consultation on vital courses of action taking place between the federal government, the employers' federation and the trade unions. Legal stipulations requiring this sort of consultation exist under

---

3. European Industrial Relations Review, No. 81, October 1980. It should be noted that the policy statement on new technology has been "shelved", failing ratification by the CBI member companies.

the Stability and Growth Act of 1967. For co-operation between government, labour and capital at a supra-firm level and the development of labour market and industrial policies, the relatively high degree of centralisation of these institutions has been conducive. Moreover, the philosophy of the trade unions towards labour involvement in the management of enterprises, as well as on regional and national economic decision-making, has significantly contributed to the practice of consultation. The unions have tended to view jobs and job opportunities as a kind of "social capital", the management of which should be subject to control by the major social groups. While the institutions of co-determination, at the firm as well as at the supra-firm level, have not been developed as far as the unions have called for, there is by international comparison a significant degree of de facto participation of labour in employment policies.

CONTENT OF THE DISCUSSIONS

At this point we are interested in exploring the role of participation in affecting the content of the decisions that are involved in economic restructuring and worker displacement. Starting with the highest level decisions first, capital and key plant decisions, we will consider a series of subject areas, including programmes for worker readjustment.

Business decisions - Generally speaking, unions and/or workers' representatives are not involved in business decisions, except to the extent outlined above for Germany (and to some extent this pattern also applies to Scandinavian countries). In some countries, such as the United Kingdom, unions would like to be much more involved by having parity representation on boards, but this has not taken place.

Even in Germany, many union leaders feel that the co-determination machinery at the company and plant level has turned out to be of limited value in combating the social and economic consequences of rationalisation to the worker. At best, works councillors have managed to cushion the impact of the technical and organisational changes on earnings or to provide compensation for loss of job or position in the plant. (Thus, the involvement has served the purpose of adjustment, not modification of business decisions.)

A number of unions have called for indicative planning, that is, the spelling out of long-term goals and implementation arrangements. Naturally, unions and worker representatives would like to know the direction of the business and to have this elaborated in some type of document which they can examine and discuss. While there have been many efforts to move businesses in this direction, very little has emerged.

Our view is that the emphasis on achieving co-decision authority over investment decisions is misplaced. The critical benefit of participation for unions and workers is an awareness and an opportunity to confront impending decisions concerning new directions for the business. This does not require parity representation but requires the presence of union or worker representatives at the highest levels. Since most decisions do not get made at any one point in time or made by any one person but rather, in the modern enterprise, emerge over an extended period of time, it is important for union representatives to be in a position to know about them and to present their points of view for consideration. Participation at the highest levels can shape the speed and some of the attributes of the decision, even though the basic decision may not be reversed. Hence, we would emphasize the <u>presence</u>, not <u>parity</u>, of union representatives, and a process of <u>consultation</u>, not necessarily co-decision-making.

<u>Release of information about impending changes</u> – Currently, the Parliament of the European Economic Community is considering a piece of legislation that would require corporations to disclose their capital plans on a regular basis. Such a requirement would go far beyond the general guidelines of giving notice to workers and their representatives about changes that affect particular operations. This code, if enacted, would require the release of information concerning the shift of a company's assets from one country to another or from one line of activity to another.

While the release of information about business plans would not, in and of itself, constitute any increased participation, nevertheless, unions and worker representatives, possessing such information, would be in a much stronger position to influence the plans and to talk concretely about the consequences.

<u>Employment level agreements</u> – Unions, if they seek to bargain about employment levels, may be successful; although the nagging question remains whether such a strategy is a desirable course of action over the long run. Unions, for example in the Netherlands, have sought to bargain employment levels to ensure that a given number of workers would continue to be used in a particular undertaking. Management views the objective of setting employment levels as adversarial, to wit, the battle that took place between British Leyland and the then leader of the shop stewards' movement in that company, Derek Robinson. Ultimately, employment levels depend on the viability of the enterprise. The effort to secure a

given level of employment in the short run may result in
compounding the problem of survival over the long run. In
general, it would appear that unions can shape the timing
and the distribution of employment changes, as the unions
at Volkswagen have done on a number of occasions, but it
is not generally desirable or feasible for employment con-
trasts to be negotiated by unions.

   Enhancing the viability of the enterprise - Almost by
definition, unions are heavily involved in productivity
bargaining, rollbacks, discussions about alternate products and in developing other ways to keep the current
work force usefully employed. Where unions are absent or
weak at the plant level, such as in Japan and to some extent in France and Germany, the emergence of these subject
areas that require vital local-level union organisation
may be limited. The most numerous examples of unions
tackling these subjects come from the United States and
the United Kingdom, where there is a tradition of involved
shop-floor labour relations.

   Human resource programmes - Management takes the lead
in developing human resource plans and programmes. The
role of unions and their representatives is somewhat
limited in this area. As we indicated earlier, unions do
not derive very much in the way of explicit gains from such
programmes. It is in Germany where the subject is most
developed and where labour representatives are involved
through the mechanism of co-determination, and we present
at this point some lessons from the practice of human
resource planning in a number of firms in that country.

   Under the revised Plant Constitution Act of 1972 in
Germany, the works councils have rights of information,
consultation and co-determination in matters of personnel
planning on the firm and plant level. The general idea
for this participation of worker representatives was to
counterbalance the principle of pure profit maximisation
in the employment policies of enterprises and to place
greater weight on worker needs and interests in decision-
making. Both trade unions and employers agreed to this
principle of co-operation in a statement made in the
course of joint consultation of employers, unions and the
Minister of Labour in 1970.

   While there have been demonstrations of clear-cut
improvements in the rationality of employment policies of
firms, joint planning has led to a longer-run orientation
in the policies and to more socially acceptable ways of
work force reduction: there has also been disenchantment
with respect to what personnel planning at the enterprise
level can achieve. In some quarters the works councils,
after having gone through the experience of involvement
in work force reduction, have reached the conclusion that
it might be better to stay away from any involvement in
"managing the reduction", since in effect they had become

collaborators in activities over which they had only limited discretion.

From experience, there are at least three lessons that have been learned about the requirements necessary for making the participation of labour on the enterprise level work:

    i) Personnel planning at the firm level cannot eliminate work force reduction as such. It cannot influence economic fluctuations or international product cycles and redevelopment. Thus, joint personnel policies at the enterprise level can only be part of multi-level policies to deal with employment problems.

    ii) At the enterprise level, the top executive has to take responsibilities in personnel planning. It is at the top level that basic conflicts between goals are resolved.

    iii) To give sufficient weight to social considerations, labour representatives have to enter the decision-making process at the formative and planning stage. Among other things, this means that they have to become aware of investment decisions. Frustration among works councillors arises when they are heavily involved in the implementation phase of work force reduction, but have little or no participation in the formative stage of business policies. This problem, in part, stems from the structures of participation specified by law which allows for far-reaching rights of co-determination for works councils in the later implementation stage and less and weaker rights in the formative stages.

Worker readjustment programmes - The best examples of union involvement in helping shape and operate programmes for worker adjustment come out of the United States, where there has been a tradition going back to the Armour Automation Committee of the 1950s down to the present time when companies readily bargain over the impact of economic change and willingly involve the unions in the implementation process in order to cushion the impact of the change for the workers involved.

One of the authors of the present report was involved in a formal labour-management committee that applied some of the principles of the Armour Automation Fund to the public sector for some 10,000 workers who had been made redundant by the State of New York during the early and mid-1970s. Using a variety of techniques such as retraining, relocation and counselling, the committee initiated a series of programmes that made it possible for workers to regain employment with the state in other positions and, in a limited number of cases, to move to the private sector.

In other countries, such as the United Kingdom, the operation of these transition programmes is primarily in the hands of the government agencies and the corporations involved. This is particularly true for British Steel: it also describes the auspices for readjustment programmes in France and Germany.

In the case of Germany, the role of the union has been to influence the transfer arrangements - even though unions view the worker readjustment phase as the last line of defence, with their primary interest focusing on preventing the displacements by being in a position to influence the overall shape of business plans. However, in view of the limited effectiveness of the co-determination system, unions have tried to reach industry-wide agreements not just to compensate workers for losses or disadvantages, but to avert changes in the production system which show detrimental effects for the workers in terms of skill level, wages and job security. In other words, by a new generation of agreements, unions have attempted to exert an influence directly on the number and quality of jobs.

The most significant agreements of this kind were concluded in the printing industry and in the metal industry of North-Württemberg/North Baden. The agreements include provisions for preferential assignment of displaced workers, protection from downgrading and partial wage guarantees. The ultimate objective of the union, which was to fix the average level of pay grades of the work force, was not, however, attained.

VIII

PRINCIPLES OF INTEGRATIVE ADJUSTMENT

STRUCTURAL ADJUSTMENT:
BOTH AN OLD AND A NEW QUESTION

"For the promotion of the fundamental economic and
social objectives of continuing economic growth
and rising living standards for the population, it
is important that these innovations be made as
smoothly as possible with due consideration of the
people involved. Policy-makers and administrators
of an active manpower policy are therefore chal-
lenged to design policies, programmes, services
and aids which will convert negative or resisting
attitudes into positive or supporting ones. To
achieve this objective both the initiators of
change and the policy-makers should be conversant
with workers' attitudes toward change and the
tools available for realising a positive attitude
and behaviour."(1)

This statement was written by Solomon Barkin in an introductory note to an integrated survey published by OECD
in 1965. This survey took up the question of how to respond to the advance of mechanisation and automation in
the then rapidly expanding mass production industries and
the concomitant problems of fragmentation of work, social
disintegration, loss of employment and loss of worker
control arising in the course of this process.

Barkin's statement is still valid for today's problems. Whether change is accepted or not depends, after
all, on how the changes are brought about, who is involved, and what the distribution of risks, costs and
gains from the changes are. The way of doing it and the
cui bono are still the most crucial issues involved in
major structural transformations. In this sense, periods

---

1. A. Touraine and Associates, Workers' Attitudes to
Technical Change, OECD, Paris, 1965, p. 7.

of major changes are alike and it is useful to recall the insights and experiences from past episodes of structural adjustments.

Yet there are also novel elements in each phase of structural change. The nature and scale of the problem have changed. Today, more than ever before, a global process of redivision of labour is at the root of the adjustment process. And the magnitude of employment which is at risk in national economies through structural adjustment is tremendous. For example, the automobile industry in Europe which has been threatened by Japanese imports makes up one-tenth of total industrial production. Automobiles account for between 8 and 12 per cent of total exports of the European Economic Community. Total direct employment is two million workers. If the supplier industry is included, more than eight million jobs in the EEC depend on automobile production. Moreover, the social institutions, the actors involved and the level of expectation and courses of action considered legitimate are different from the 1960s.

The old solutions are no longer adequate and need to be complemented or redeveloped. To a large extent the seeming intractability of today's problems stems from the limited usefulness of previous solutions – the policies, rules and institutional networks developed in the 1950s and 1960s to cope with adjustment problems. It is not sufficient to extend, intensify or improve previous policies and measures, or, in other words, to develop existing policies in a linear and more comprehensive fashion, in order to resolve new crises. New instruments and new social organisations are needed for an effective solution. While the social challenges raised by the spread of mass production methods could be confronted within a national organisational framework, the issues raised by a worldwide redivision of labour, by their very nature, require trans-national ways of dealing with them. There are both substantive policies as well as organisational arrangements which tend to be unique to each major cycle of change.

An essential ingredient of any effective solution is first to achieve an adequate understanding of the variables which are of key importance to structural change. In this regard there seem to be a number of misperceptions. When it comes to explaining why some countries seem to cope better than others with the current employment crisis, the arguments put forward frequently have a very subjective slant. The ultimate explanation for the differences is sought in personality traits of workers or in their openness or willingness to accept innovations. While the British worker is regarded as "bloody-minded", being very resistant to any kind of change, the Japanese worker is, in the view of many analysts, extremely docile, disciplined and willing to accept any change introduced

and the hardships associated with it. This attitudinal
and behavioural uniqueness is, moreover, often related to
some exotic cultural elements inherent in the Japanese
family and other pre-industrial social institutions.

This type of subjective explanation not only fails
to account for significant changes within relatively short
periods of time in a country's productivity, competitiveness and capacity to master new challenges - one should
assume that personal or cultural traits are more stable
and enduring - but also disregards the interconnection
between worker behaviour and the social organisation
within which processes of change take place.

We feel that it is still the social organisation
which is the decisive variable responsible for how change
comes about, whether suddenly and abruptly like natural
disasters or smoothly and deliberately. And it is,
furthermore, dependent on the social organisation how the
risks and gains are distributed among the principal
groups. Both are decisive for the question of acceptability of structural change. The main balance to be
accomplished by the organisation of change is one between
the kind and speed of change, on the one hand, and the
security, rights and needs of workers and the needs of
communities, on the other hand.

GOALS AND STANDARDS FOR CHANGE

There are a multitude of goals by which structural
change should be guided or which should be regarded as
minimum requirements for effective solutions to structural adjustment. We believe that these goals should
include aggregate full employment in the longer run;
depending on market conditions and productivity trends,
improvement or at least maintenance of the level of wages,
working conditions and fair labour standards; and
finally, improvement or at least maintenance of the quality of work. These objectives should be obtained by the
participation and co-operation of the major groups in
the productive process in an attempt to resolve conflicts
and avoid industrial warfare.

Many OECD countries have, by now, written statements
including these goals in their national labour market or
employment policies. For example, Section Two of the
German Labour Promotion Act lists as objectives of public
labour market policies:

   - to prevent unemployment and under-utilisation
     of skills and qualifications of the labour
     force;

- to secure and improve the occupational mobility of labour;
- to avoid, compensate and eliminate disadvantages for workers from technical and economic structural change;
- to promote the integration of physically, mentally and psychically handicapped persons;
- to promote the integration of women, aged workers and other disadvantaged worker groups;
- to improve the regional and industrial structure of employment.

These quantitative and qualitative objectives of employment policies should be seen as points of orientation as well as standards within which active solutions to employment problems are reached. They should be defined or applied not only within local or national limits, but should be extended to an international scale.

The shift of employment from the old to the new countries along with a redivision of labour would be questionable if the competitive advantages of the production in new countries is built on the exploitation of a weak, non-organised labour force, on excessive working hours, and on the use of child labour. Unions in the industrialised nations have come to resent this type of unfair competition. In 1979, the leaders of the world's free trade unions called for "social clauses" in trade agreements. Earlier, in 1976, the World Employment Conference stated that "the competitiveness of new imports from developing countries should not be achieved to the detriment of fair labour standards". We believe that as yet, there is little progress to ensure that international standards of fair labour will be maintained.

Solutions can be seen as improper that cut down unemployment in one country at the expense of higher unemployment in another, thus merely shifting the problem across national boundaries. Goal definition and goal attainment should be applied, not narrowly, but on a global scale. This is not an illusory or idealistic conception, but can be understood in the context of mutual interests and gains. Thus, for example, the strategy of advanced technology and modernisation of the economies as applied by the mature industrial nations will only be successful if there is sufficient inducement, buying power and financial strength on the part of the less advanced or younger industrial countries in order to allow them to acquire the advanced products. Thus, the advanced countries must take into consideration and allow for positive conditions for development in the countries which are newcomers to the industrial scene.

CO-ORDINATION AND INTEGRATION OF POLICIES, POLICY-MAKING AND IMPLEMENTATION

To elaborate and enhance policy instruments for handling employment dislocation situations is one major task. Another one, possibly even more urgent and effective, is the integration of policies and measures into more comprehensive and coherent strategies and the co-ordination of policy-making and implementation at various administrative levels.

1. <u>Horizontal integration and co-ordination of employment and employment-related policies</u>. Many different policies bear more or less directly and explicitly on employment: fiscal, economic, structural, regional, industrial, technology, education and training policies. In many countries the jurisdiction or responsibility for the creation and administration of these policies rests with different agencies and groups. Both the goal-setting and the effect of the instruments are not always consistent. The policies were frequently formed in response to some very specific sub-problem. Often there is no co-ordination of these policies in terms of an integrated and comprehensive strategy.

2. <u>The need for vertical integration and co-ordination</u>. Vertical integration refers to the substantive and procedural co-ordination of employment policies between different institutional or administrative levels:

- across different levels within institutions or organisations, such as different levels of governments, public employment offices, trade unions and employers;
- across different levels of policy formulation and decision-making bodies.

Improvement in co-ordination may be expected from joint local or regional <u>task forces or labour market conferences</u> which include representation of enterprises, unions, communities, government and the employment offices. The task force or conference would be assigned the task of developing on a local or regional level medium-term employment concepts, drawing from existing proposals as well as the given public employment programmes and instruments.

The potential effectiveness of these task forces or conferences would not primarily concern new policies, but rather lie in being more responsive to the particular local or regional conditions and to the different needs and capacities of local actors and agencies. This procedure would be more workable than having pre-fixed and rather general and inflexible solutions offered by governments, which have little potential for being adjusted and, thereby, have a "take-it-or-leave-it" character. In effect, in practice this will mean some decentralisation of policy-making and implementation. This should be regarded as an important complement to the need for co-operation on a centralised (international) level that is required from the globalised nature of economic problems.

THE LEVEL FOR POLICY-MAKING AND CONFLICT RESOLUTION

The proper level at which problems and conflicts of dislocation are to be resolved is a very crucial variable; it deserves at least as much attention as the type of policies to be applied. An argument can be made that, with the shift in the nature of competition, a corresponding shift in the organisational structure of policy-making has to be made to deal effectively with the social outcomes and adverse effects of competition. More specifically, it can be argued that under the present conditions of low overall economic growth and considerable decline of key industries in many countries, the capacity for decentralised problem and conflict resolution, i.e. resolution at the enterprise level, has narrowed; and that the solution is to be found by more centralised policy-making, i.e. policies on national and international levels in line with the more internationalised nature of competition.

A more centralised containment and resolution seems to be indicated as long as co-operative solutions are to be found. Under the condition of shrinking markets and fierce competition, a winner-loser situation is very likely to emerge if the competition remains unconstrained. The winner-loser outcome is not very satisfactory, even for the surviving firm or country; for long-run opportunity for growth in all countries depends very much on the development of international trade. A decline in trade will hit everyone, the only difference being in the timing.

During the period of significant economic growth in Western countries after World War II, there had been a tendency for decentralisation of the industrial relations systems. In part, this tendency resulted from the spread and consolidation of enterprise internal labour markets, internalising the major labour market functions of allocation, training and pricing of labour. Along with this shift, the company or the plant became the major locus of conflict and conflict resolution; and correspondingly, both employer and union organisation showed tendencies towards decentralisation with the powerful organisational representation residing in the plant. Major instruments of employment policy have been developed at the company or plant level, such as <u>personnel planning</u>. This is an adequate response as long as the problems of excess labour and redundancy, if and where they occur, are limited to a few firms or industries and can be absorbed by sufficient demand for labour elsewhere in the economy.

The contexts for effective policies are fundamentally different if dislocation occurs on a large scale and if the prospects for displaced workers (to be reintegrated by the growth sector) are poor. In this situation, enterprises face limited capacity to deal with the problems effectively and satisfactorily from a social point of view. They can still contribute to positive remedial action by cushioning the adverse consequences of work force reduction. And they can make increased efforts for restructuring. But this by itself is unlikely to eliminate unemployment.

If, as is the case at present, large-scale dislocation in key industries cannot be resolved by a decentralised economic order, national economic and social interests are at stake and the problem becomes very much a concern for national governments. It becomes likely that the situation is perceived as one in which national economies compete against each other.

A crossroads situation for strategic responses emerges in this situation. Governments can choose between nationalist (unco-operative) and international (co-operative) solutions. Both protectionist and the mercantilist strategy of subsidisation to improve the competitive position of a particular country can be seen in this light as narrow nationalist strategies, with very large potentials and risks for harmful effects in the future.

The European steel industry demonstrates how non-co-ordinated extensive subsidisation to production through national governments can create large over-capacity and thereby increase international competition with the risk of more protectionism to come. If, as has been the case, all countries in a stagnating or declining market promote the modernisation of steel production without cutting out capacity and if the improvement of productivity can only be achieved through technical means that lead to increased capacity, then a kind of "rat-race" competition is likely to occur.

A second predicament under which centralisation of bargaining and policy-making may become necessary (and has already become visible) is the growing role of multinational companies in world markets. As typified by the world car, multinational companies can quickly shift production across countries in reaction to changes in production costs and other considerations of flexibility

in "sourcing". This flexibility poses problems of a different sort and scale. As the relocation of production
facilities can often have large employment effects, significant local or regional dislocation may arise. A
second problem is posed for trade unions, who tend to see
their bargaining position undermined, given the regional
or, at best, national reach of collective agreements.
Under these circumstances unions will be forced to adopt
an international outlook and develop more international
organisation in order to counter the cross-national flexibility of multinational companies. In industries like
chemicals and automobiles, moves have been made by trade
unions from affected countries to develop some co-ordinated
counter-strategies.

While there is a clear need for the co-ordination of
industrial and employment policies at an international
level, there is also a need for centralisation at national
level. The need is the greater the more decentralised
and fractionalised is the national political and industrial relations order. Centralisation is required to
avert ruinous competition among states and municipalities
to attract new business and employment through tax abate-
ment, subsidies and other financial inducements, and
where the luring away merely means a corresponding loss
of employment elsewhere. A centralised industrial policy
can prevent a "beggar thy neighbour" situation.

THE INTEGRATIVE APPROACH AS AN ALTERNATIVE TO PROTECTIONIST THINKING

In order to maintain and extend the economic and
social standards achieved so far through technological
progress and development to trade, the avenues to structural change should not be foreclosed. This requires the
industrial countries to find constructive ways out of the
present economic slump and protectionist mood; it also
requires further contraction of employment in many traditional sectors in the advanced countries to accommodate
the new industrial capacity of the developing countries.
Turning away from this premise would mean shutting off
the prospect of significant mutual gains from this co-
operation in the future and would aggravate the risk of
further divergence and conflict between the Northern and
Southern hemispheres.(2)

---

2. North-South: A Program for Survival, The Report
of the Independent Commission on International Development
Issues (under the chairmanship of W. Brandt), The MIT
Press, 1980, p. 177.

A major obstacle to achieving economic progress has become the divergent conditions between the industrialised nations. Thus, the difference in strategy between the countries taking a forward-planning or offensive stance versus the ones turning more towards defence and conservatism can to a large extent be traced to differences in basic economic conditions. A country like Japan leans more towards the attacking approach of restructuring because it needs large incomes from exports to make good for the poor terms of trade as a result of a lack of energy and raw materials. Thus, it is a natural candidate for a free trade policy in exports. In addition, it does not suffer, as yet, from very high unemployment which is likely to raise resistance to structural change. In contrast, the United States meets more resistance to change due to pockets of high regional unemployment, but it can also afford more easily a reduction in international trade due to much larger domestic product markets.

There is further the question of whether a country with a large proportion of its industry sheltered from international competition can reasonably choose an attacking strategy of restructuring. Britain, for example, would risk losing a significant proportion of employment if it would suddenly scrap public support to various industries and protection of employment. Adjustment in industry was already lagging in the 1960s. Slow growth has further reduced the contribution of the production sector; deindustrialisation has continued after the oil crisis of 1973. More recently, regional and national unemployment has been rising to very high levels and many cases of serious dislocation are occurring simultaneously.

At the same time it is clear that continued subsidisation of the troubled industries in many nations, without plans and timetables for reduction, will run the danger not only of extending the life of non-competitive and very costly operations but, as is indicated at present in parts of the European auto and steel industries, may also lead to further over-capacities and consequently to very painful or brutal solutions at some future point.

CO-ORDINATING ECONOMIC AND SOCIAL CONSIDERATIONS

Foreclosing or overly narrowing the avenues of structural change in an economy tends to engender the risk of losing international competitiveness, and this, in turn, is likely to induce a spiral of protectionism, economic isolation and lowered social security. Conversely, ignoring social and individual interests in the process of structural transition is likely to result in resistance to change and, consequently, in low productivity and reduced welfare. Thus, violation of either the

124

"economic must" or the "human ought" in the equation of
change generates more or less the same outcome, that is
the failure to achieve both economic and social progress.
Experience clearly tells us that if an initial imbalance
sets in, a cumulative aggravation of the situation is
likely to occur.

These findings bring us back to one of the key
principles of integrative adjustment: the continuous
need to balance economic and human interests in the displacement process. The economic viability of enterprises
and industries and employment standards as specified
above, must be integrated in a coherent policy.

In this report we have highlighted countries with
"best practices", that is, relatively successful approaches
towards co-ordinating economic and social needs. By
international comparison these countries exhibit most of
the principles of integrative adjustment. On the other
hand, we do not want to suggest that there is one, and
only one, "best solution" to the problem of abrupt dislocation. The divergence of economic and social pre-
conditions both within and between countries is too
large, and "convergence" through uniform action is
neither probable nor necessarily desirable. Even within
the countries which so far appear to have fared relatively
well through the period of structural reconversion, a
variety of approaches across industries can be observed.

In line with the stated principle of sectional and
regional responsiveness of policy solutions, one may
claim that the task of co-ordinating economic and human
imperatives may be accomplished by different strategies
and measures with equivalent results emerging. In some
instances, this co-ordination can best be realised
through co-operative arrangements on a national or international level. Sometimes it may not be a plan, but a
synchronisation of actions of management and labour in a
way which allows the two objectives to be reconciled.
In some instances, government may be involved (as is the
case with the European steel industry), in other cases the
government may not be actively involved and the linkage
will be directly between top management and labour
leaders (as is happening in the US automobile industry).
Thus, what we advocate is that, given widely varying
market and institutional frameworks both between and
within national economies, industries and firms, there
should be flexibility in political responses to dislocation within the general boundaries of integrative
adjustment principles.

OECD SALES AGENTS
DÉPOSITAIRES DES PUBLICATIONS DE L'OCDE

ARGENTINA – ARGENTINE
Carlos Hirsch S.R.L., Florida 165, 4° Piso (Galería Guemes)
1333 BUENOS AIRES, Tel. 33.1787.2391 y 30.7122
AUSTRALIA – AUSTRALIE
Australia and New Zealand Book Company Pty, Ltd.,
10 Aquatic Drive, Frenchs Forest, N.S.W. 2086
P.O. Box 459, BROOKVALE, N.S.W. 2100
AUSTRIA – AUTRICHE
OECD Publications and Information Center
4 Simrockstrasse 5300 BONN. Tel. (0228) 21.60.45
Local Agent/Agent local :
Gerold and Co., Graben 31, WIEN 1. Tel. 52.22.35
BELGIUM – BELGIQUE
CCLS – LCLS
19, rue Plantin, 1070 BRUXELLES. Tel. 02.521.04.73
BRAZIL – BRÉSIL
Mestre Jou S.A., Rua Guaipa 518,
Caixa Postal 24090, 05089 SAO PAULO 10. Tel. 261.1920
Rua Senador Dantas 19 s/205-6, RIO DE JANEIRO GB.
Tel. 232.07.32
CANADA
Renouf Publishing Company Limited,
2182 St. Catherine Street West,
MONTRÉAL, Que. H3H 1M7. Tel. (514)937.3519
OTTAWA, Ont. K1P 5A6, 61 Sparks Street
DENMARK – DANEMARK
Munksgaard Export and Subscription Service
35, Nørre Søgade
DK 1370 KØBENHAVN K. Tel. +45.1.12.85.70
FINLAND – FINLANDE
Akateeminen Kirjakauppa
Keskuskatu 1, 00100 HELSINKI 10. Tel. 65.11.22
FRANCE
Bureau des Publications de l'OCDE,
2 rue André-Pascal, 75775 PARIS CEDEX 16. Tel. (1) 524.81.67
Principal correspondant :
13602 AIX-EN-PROVENCE : Librairie de l'Université.
Tel. 26.18.08
GERMANY – ALLEMAGNE
OECD Publications and Information Center
4 Simrockstrasse 5300 BONN Tel. (0228) 21.60.45
GREECE – GRÈCE
Librairie Kauffmann, 28 rue du Stade,
ATHÈNES 132. Tel. 322.21.60
HONG-KONG
Government Information Services,
Publications/Sales Section, Baskerville House,
2/F., 22 Ice House Street
ICELAND – ISLANDE
Snaebjörn Jónsson and Co., h.f.,
Hafnarstraeti 4 and 9, P.O.B. 1131, REYKJAVIK.
Tel. 13133/14281/11936
INDIA – INDE
Oxford Book and Stationery Co. :
NEW DELHI-1, Scindia House. Tel. 45896
CALCUTTA 700016, 17 Park Street. Tel. 240832
INDONESIA – INDONÉSIE
PDIN-LIPI, P.O. Box 3065/JKT., JAKARTA, Tel. 583467
IRELAND – IRLANDE
TDC Publishers – Library Suppliers
12 North Frederick Street, DUBLIN 1 Tel. 744835-749677
ITALY – ITALIE
Libreria Commissionaria Sansoni :
Via Lamarmora 45, 50121 FIRENZE. Tel. 579751/584468
Via Bartolini 29, 20155 MILANO. Tel. 365083
Sub-depositari :
Ugo Tassi
Via A. Farnese 28, 00192 ROMA. Tel. 310590
Editrice e Libreria Herder,
Piazza Montecitorio 120, 00186 ROMA. Tel. 6794628
Costantino Ercolano, Via Generale Orsini 46, 80132 NAPOLI. Tel.
405210
Libreria Hoepli, Via Hoepli 5, 20121 MILANO. Tel. 865446
Libreria Scientifica, Dott. Lucio de Biasio "Aeiou"
Via Meravigli 16, 20123 MILANO Tel. 807679
Libreria Zanichelli
Piazza Galvani 1/A, 40124 Bologna Tel. 237389
Libreria Lattes, Via Garibaldi 3, 10122 TORINO. Tel. 519274
La diffusione delle edizioni OCSE è inoltre assicurata dalle migliori
librerie nelle città più importanti.
JAPAN – JAPON
OECD Publications and Information Center,
Landic Akasaka Bldg., 2-3-4 Akasaka,
Minato-ku, TOKYO 107 Tel. 586.2016
KOREA – CORÉE
Pan Korea Book Corporation,
P.O. Box n° 101 Kwangwhamun, SÉOUL. Tel. 72.7369

LEBANON – LIBAN
Documenta Scientifica/Redico,
Edison Building, Bliss Street, P.O. Box 5641, BEIRUT.
Tel. 354429 – 344425
MALAYSIA – MALAISIE
and/et **SINGAPORE - SINGAPOUR**
University of Malaya Co-operative Bookshop Ltd.
P.O. Box 1127, Jalan Pantai Baru
KUALA LUMPUR. Tel. 51425, 54058, 54361
THE NETHERLANDS – PAYS-BAS
Staatsuitgeverij
Verzendboekhandel Chr. Plantijnstraat 1
Postbus 20014
2500 EA S-GRAVENHAGE. Tel. nr. 070.789911
Voor bestellingen: Tel. 070.789208
NEW ZEALAND – NOUVELLE-ZÉLANDE
Publications Section,
Government Printing Office Bookshops:
AUCKLAND: Retail Bookshop: 25 Rutland Street,
Mail Orders: 85 Beach Road, Private Bag C.P.O.
HAMILTON: Retail Ward Street,
Mail Orders, P.O. Box 857
WELLINGTON: Retail: Mulgrave Street (Head Office),
Cubacade World Trade Centre
Mail Orders: Private Bag
CHRISTCHURCH: Retail: 159 Hereford Street,
Mail Orders: Private Bag
DUNEDIN: Retail: Princes Street
Mail Order: P.O. Box 1104
NORWAY – NORVÈGE
J.G. TANUM A/S Karl Johansgate 43
P.O. Box 1177 Sentrum OSLO 1. Tel. (02) 80.12.60
PAKISTAN
Mirza Book Agency, 65 Shahrah Quaid-E-Azam, LAHORE 3.
Tel. 66839
PHILIPPINES
National Book Store, Inc.
Library Services Division, P.O. Box 1934, MANILA.
Tel. Nos. 49.43.06 to 09, 40.53.45, 49.45.12
PORTUGAL
Livraria Portugal, Rua do Carmo 70-74,
1117 LISBOA CODEX. Tel. 360582/3
SPAIN – ESPAGNE
Mundi-Prensa Libros, S.A.
Castelló 37, Apartado 1223, MADRID-1. Tel. 275.46.55
Libreria Bosch, Ronda Universidad 11, BARCELONA 7.
Tel. 317.53.08, 317.53.58
SWEDEN – SUÈDE
AB CE Fritzes Kungl Hovbokhandel,
Box 16 356, S 103 27 STH, Regeringsgatan 12,
DS STOCKHOLM. Tel. 08/23.89.00
SWITZERLAND – SUISSE
OECD Publications and Information Center
4 Simrockstrasse 5300 BONN. Tel. (0228) 21.60.45
Local Agents/Agents locaux
Librairie Payot, 6 rue Grenus, 1211 GENÈVE 11. Tel. 022.31.89.50
TAIWAN – FORMOSE
Good Faith Worldwide Int'l Co., Ltd.
9th floor, No. 118, Sec. 2
Chung Hsiao E. Road
TAIPEI. Tel. 391.7396/391.7397
THAILAND – THAILANDE
Suksit Siam Co., Ltd., 1715 Rama IV Rd,
Samyan, BANGKOK 5. Tel. 2511630
TURKEY – TURQUIE
Kültur Yayinlari Is-Türk Ltd. Sti.
Atatürk Bulvari No : 77/B
KIZILAY/ANKARA. Tel. 17 02 66
Dolmabahce Cad. No : 29
BESIKTAS/ISTANBUL. Tel. 60 71 88
UNITED KINGDOM – ROYAUME-UNI
H.M. Stationery Office, P.O.B. 569,
LONDON SE1 9NH. Tel. 01.928.6977, Ext. 410 or
49 High Holborn, LONDON WC1V 6 HB (personal callers)
Branches at: EDINBURGH, BIRMINGHAM, BRISTOL,
MANCHESTER, BELFAST.
UNITED STATES OF AMERICA – ÉTATS-UNIS
OECD Publications and Information Center, Suite 1207,
1750 Pennsylvania Ave., N.W. WASHINGTON, D.C.20006 – 4582
Tel. (202) 724.1857
VENEZUELA
Libreria del Este, Avda. F. Miranda 52, Edificio Galipan,
CARACAS 106. Tel. 32.23.01/33.26.04/33.24.73
YUGOSLAVIA – YOUGOSLAVIE
Jugoslovenska Knjiga, Terazije 27, P.O.B. 36, BEOGRAD.
Tel. 621.992

Les commandes provenant de pays où l'OCDE n'a pas encore désigné de dépositaire peuvent être adressées à :
OCDE, Bureau des Publications, 2, rue André-Pascal, 75775 PARIS CEDEX 16.

Orders and inquiries from countries where sales agents have not yet been appointed may be sent to:
OECD, Publications Office, 2 rue André-Pascal, 75775 PARIS CEDEX 16.

65958-12-1982

OECD PUBLICATIONS, 2, rue André-Pascal, 75775 PARIS CEDEX 16 - No. 42437 1983
PRINTED IN FRANCE
(81 83 01 1) ISBN 92-64-12408-X